THE RECORD OF A REGIMENT OF THE LINE

BEING

A REGIMENTAL HISTORY OF THE 1st BATTALION DEVONSHIRE REGIMENT DURING THE BOER WAR

1899–1902

BY COLONEL M. JACSON

The Naval & Military Press Ltd

Published by
The Naval & Military Press Ltd
Unit 10, Ridgewood Industrial Park,
Uckfield, East Sussex,
TN22 5QE England
Tel: +44 (0) 1825 749494
Fax: +44 (0) 1825 765701
www.naval-military-press.com

© The Naval & Military Press Ltd 2004

In reprinting in facsimile from the original, any imperfections are inevitably reproduced and the quality may fall short of modern type and cartographic standards.

MONUMENT ERECTED TO OFFICERS AND MEN OF THE DEVONSHIRE REGIMENT WHO FELL ON JANUARY 6TH ON WAGON HILL, SIEGE OF LADYSMITH

Frontispiece

CONTENTS

CHAPTER		PAGE
I.	EVENTS LEADING UP TO THE SIEGE OF LADYSMITH	1
II.	SIEGE OF LADYSMITH	30
III.	EVENTS FOLLOWING THE SIEGE OF LADYSMITH, AND THE ADVANCE NORTH UNDER SIR REDVERS BULLER	104
IV.	LYDENBURG	149
V.	TREKKING IN THE NORTH-EAST TRANSVAAL	176

LIST OF ILLUSTRATIONS

Monument erected to Officers and Men of the Devonshire Regiment who fell on January 6th on Wagon Hill, Siege of Ladysmith	*Frontispiece*
	FACE PAGE
En route to Ladysmith	5
In the Trenches, Ladysmith	36
Town Hall, Ladysmith, Clock-tower damaged by Shell Fire	44
After a Wet Night in the Traverses, Ladysmith	56
The Railway Bridge, with Cæsar's Camp in distance, Ladysmith	62
Lieut.-Colonel C. W. Park	66
Naval Battery Hill, Ladysmith	
Monument erected to Devons on Wagon Hill, on spot where the charge took place, Ladysmith	70
A Peaceful Sunday	80
Devon Officers remaining fit for duty at the end of the Siege	102
Brigadier-General Walter Kitchener	104

LIST OF ILLUSTRATIONS

	FACE PAGE
Railway Bridge destroyed by Boers, Ingagane	108
Making Barbed-wire Entanglement, Ingagane	110
The Baggage of General Buller's Army crossing Beginderlyn Bridge	116
Trekking with General Buller	124
Devons crossing the Sabi River	140
Colonel C. W. Park, Mission Camp, Lydenburg	148
Wire Bridge, Lydenburg	160
Mission Camp Fort, Lydenburg (interior)	170
Remains of Boer Big Gun, Waterval	180
Crossing the Steelport River	182
Dawn — after a Night March, Trichardtsfontein	200
Devons en route to Durban	208
Monument erected in Ladysmith Cemetery	218

MAPS

Siege of Ladysmith	*End of Volume*
Natal and S.E. Transvaal	,,

PREFACE

BY LIEUT.-GENERAL W. KITCHENER

EXPERIENCE we all know to be a valuable asset, and experience in war is the most costly of its kind. To enable those coming after us to reconstruct the picture of war, Regimental Histories have proved of infinite value. That such a record fills a sentimental want hardly requires assertion.

My first feelings on being honoured with a request from the Devonshire Regiment to write a preface to the account of their "Work in South Africa, 1899–1902," were, I confess, How could I refuse so difficult a task gracefully? However, on further consideration it seemed to me that undoubtedly such a preface should be written by some one outside the corps itself. Onlookers, as the saying goes, often see most of the game, and, being free from personal bias, can often add something to what those engrossed in the meshes of life's details can only appreciate from a narrower point of view.

From this standpoint, and as I was the General under whom the 1st Devons served longest in South Africa, it seemed obviously my duty to attempt the task.

The "Work of the 1st Battalion of the Devonshire Regiment" is portrayed in these pages. It therefore only remains for me to add, for the benefit of coming generations, what manner of men these were, who by their dogged devotion to duty helped to overcome the Boer. Associated as one was with many corps in the close intimacy of veldt life, it was a study of the deepest interest to note the individuality that characterized each, and which was often as clearly and as well defined as that of the men with whom one daily came in contact.

During the many months of our intimate association, and in the varied situations that presented themselves, I cannot call to mind any single occasion on which the Devons were ever flurried or even hurried. Their imperturbability of temper, even under the most trying conditions, could not be surpassed.

Another characteristic of the corps was its inherent thrift. They were, in fact, essentially a "self-help" corps. When a flood came and washed away the bridge leading to the picket line, no sapper was required to show them how to throw a suspension bridge above the flood from tree to cliff. It was characteristic of the Regiment that they carried out in war their peace training, never allowing the atmosphere of excitement to distort their actions.

If we take Elandslaagte, Wagon Hill, or any of the hundred and one ticklish night operations in which they took part, this trait will be ever noteworthy, that they acted as was to be expected of them, and made no fuss of having done so.

We have all read realistic descriptions of troops on the march in South Africa, the writer using all his cunning to depict the war-worn dirty condition of his heroes, seeming to glean satisfaction from their grease-stained khaki. It must be admitted that the South African War is responsible for a somewhat changed condition of thought as regards cleanliness and its relation to smartness. No such abstraction disturbed the Devons; a Devon man was always clean. Individuals of some corps could be readily identified by their battered helmets or split boots; not so the Devons. No helmet badge was necessary for their identification, and the veriest tyro could not fail to recognize at any time the crisply washed Indian helmet cover.

It may be open to question whether it is for good or for evil that we should broaden our views of what goes to make a smart and useful fighting man, but the regimental system of the Devons was for no innovation of a careless go-as-you-please style. I thus lay stress on the individuality of the Devons in South Africa, because it was this individuality of theirs, born of their regimental system, which enabled them to claim so full a share in the success of that long-drawn-out campaign.

PREFACE

No one can quite appreciatively follow the story of the work of the Devons, unless he realizes the intense feeling of comradeship that animates these West-country men. To work with Devonshire men is to realize in the flesh the intensity of the local county loyalty so graphically depicted by Charles Kingsley in his *Westward Ho!* and other novels.

In conclusion, let me add, a more determined crew I never wish to see, and a better regiment to back his orders a General can never hope to have.

DALHOUSIE, *May*, 1906.

PREFACE

BY THE AUTHOR

THE story as told is an everyday account and a record of the work of the men of the 1st Battalion Devonshire Regiment during the South African War.

It exemplifies the devotion to duty, the stubbornness in adversity, and the great fighting qualities of the West-country man, which qualities existed in the time of Drake, and which still exist.

A repeating of their history of the past, a record of the present, and an example for the generation to come.

THE RECORD OF A REGIMENT OF THE LINE

CHAPTER I

EVENTS LEADING UP TO THE SIEGE OF LADYSMITH

1899

ON returning from the North-West Frontier of India at the close of the Tirah Expedition, 1897–8, the 1st Battalion Devonshire Regiment, which had served with distinction under the command of Colonel J. H. Yule in the campaign against the Afridi clans, was ordered to proceed from Peshawar to Jullunder, at which place it was quartered in 1898 and in the summer months of 1899, during which time certain companies and detachments were furnished for duty at Dalhousie, Kasauli, and Ghora Dakka (Murree Hills), and located during the hot weather at these places.

Towards the latter end of August, 1899, news from South Africa appeared ominous, and war seemed likely to break out between England and the Transvaal.

On the 8th September, 1899, confidential instructions were received from army head-quarters at Simla ordering the Regiment to get ready to move at short notice to South Africa, and a few days later further orders were received to entrain on the 16th September for Bombay *en route* to the Transvaal, which country the Regiment was destined not to reach for some months, and then only after severe fighting.

The companies quartered at Dalhousie and Ghora Dakka with difficulty joined the head-quarters at Jullunder before the 16th, and the following marches are worthy of record :—

The Dalhousie detachment marched to Pathankote, a distance of $54\frac{1}{4}$ miles, in two days. Major Curry, who was in command, gave each man a coolie for his baggage, and ordered the men to get to Duneera the first day the best way they could. At Duneera they halted for the night, and the next day pushed on in the same manner to Pathankote, where they immediately entrained and proceeded to Jullunder.

The Ghora Dakka detachment under Lieutenant Emerson marched to Rawal Pindi, a distance of fifty-four miles, in two days, and then entrained for Jullunder.

No men fell out in either party, and considering the time of year and the intense heat, they were fine performances.

Some officers were on leave in Cashmere, and only arrived at Jullunder as the Regiment was entraining.

On September 16th, 1899, the 1st Battalion Devonshire Regiment, under the command of Major C. W. Park, left Jullunder by rail for Bombay with a strength as under :—

25 officers, 1 warrant officer, and 842 sergeants, rank and file.

The following officers accompanied the battalion :—

Major C. W. Park, commanding.
Major M. C. Curry, second in command.
Captain M. G. Jacson.
Captain J. O. Travers.
Captain E. C. Wren.

Captain E. M. Morris.
Lieutenant P. H. Price-Dent.
Lieutenant J. E. I. Masterson.
Lieutenant A. F. Dalzel.
Lieutenant N. Z. Emerson.
Lieutenant G. H. I. Graham.
Lieutenant T. B. Harris.
2nd Lieutenant G. I. Watts.
2nd Lieutenant D. H. Blunt.
2nd Lieutenant H. R. Gunning.
2nd Lieutenant S. T. Hayley.
2nd Lieutenant H. W. F. Twiss.
Captain and Adjutant H. S. L. Ravenshaw.
Captain and Quartermaster H. Honner.
Warrant Officer Sergeant-Major G. E. Mitchell.

The following officers were attached for duty to the battalion :—

Major Burnside, R.A.M.C., in medical charge.
Lieutenant E. G. Caffin, Yorkshire Regiment.
Lieutenant H. W. R. Cowie, Dorset Regiment.
Lieutenant A. M. Tringham, The Queen's West Surrey Regiment.

EN ROUTE TO LADYSMITH

A REGIMENT OF THE LINE

Lieutenant J. A. Byrne, Royal Inniskilling Fusiliers.

Lieutenant E. E. M. Walker, Somersetshire Light Infantry.

The following officers were absent from the battalion on leave in England :—

Captain W. B. Lafone.
Captain G. M. Gloster.
Lieutenant H. N. Field.

Colonel J. H. Yule, commanding the battalion, was appointed to the command of the Indian Infantry Brigade, South Africa, with the temporary rank of brigadier-general. Major A. G. Spratt was placed in charge of the depot and details left at Jullunder.

The Regiment arrived without incident on September 21st at Bombay, having halted, for a few hours only, at the following places :—

On September 17th at Aligarh.
,,   ,,   18th at Jhansi.
,,   ,,   19th at Hoshangabad.
,,   ,,   20th at Deolali.

Embarkation took place immediately on arrival, the transport *Sutlej* taking five companies, head-quarters, band and drums, under Major C. W. Park; and the transport *City of London* taking three companies under Major M. C. Curry.

On the latter vessel sailed also Sir George White's Staff and the Staff of the Indian Infantry Brigade.

The *Sutlej* sailed at noon on September 21st, and it was reported that the ship was under sealed orders, and that her destination was Delagoa Bay.

The days on board were occupied in keeping the men fit with physical drill, free gymnastics, etc., and with instruction in first-aid to the wounded and the use of the field-dressing and the method of adjusting it.

On September 28th Agalega Island was sighted, and on the 30th the ship was off the east coast of Madagascar.

On the 2nd October the s.s. *Purnea* with the 60th Rifles on board was spoken, and communication by flag signal established, both vessels inquiring for news. The *Sutlej* was the last to leave port, but had nothing new to communicate.

At 7 a.m. on October 5th, in rough and

foggy weather, the *Sutlej* arrived off the coast of Africa, and the fog lifting about midday, she ran down the coastline for two hours, and arrived outside the bar at Durban.

The ships conveying the 60th Rifles and the 53rd Battery arrived an hour later. The *Sutlej* waited till 2 p.m. to enter the harbour, and arrived alongside the quay at 4 p.m., when disembarkation commenced at once in torrents of rain and heavy wind squalls.

A deputation of the Durban "West of England" Association met the Regiment on arrival and presented an address.

The first news received on landing was that war had not yet been declared, but that it was inevitable, that President Kruger had seized half a million of money on its way from Johannesburg to the Cape, and that orders had been given by him to shoot any one crossing the frontier. This may or may not have been true; a good deal of *perfectly reliable* information was being circulated about this time.

On the night of October 5th–6th the Regiment left in three trains for Ladysmith. The rain and cold caused some inconvenience to the men, as they were packed into open trucks, and obtained neither shelter nor sleep. They were new to the game then, but they saw the inside of many a coal truck later.

The journey to Pietermaritzburg was in the nature of a triumphal procession, for at various points along the line small knots of old men women and children, waving Union Jacks, cheered the troops most lustily as the trains passed.

A remark frequently heard was "How glad they are to see us," and it was evident that these people at least, who were interested and possessed homes in Natal, had not underrated the power and intentions of the Transvaal. The Regiment had an enthusiastic reception, as indeed did all troops passing to the front, flags and handkerchiefs being waved from every house farm and village. At some stations where a short stop was made to allow of other trains getting on ahead, tea and refreshments were given out free, by willing hands, to the soldiers in the trucks.

Trains were running with about 500 to 600 yards distance between them.

A REGIMENT OF THE LINE

On October 6th between 7 and 8 a.m. the trains conveying the Regiment reached Pietermaritzburg, and here the men had breakfast. Pushing on again with as little delay as possible and passing Estcourt at about 3 p.m., and Colenso about 4 p.m., Ladysmith was reached at 6 p.m.

Detraining took place at once, and the Regiment marched off to Tin Town, about two miles distant, where camp was pitched in the dark.

The infantry at this time in Ladysmith consisted of:—

The Gordon Highlanders.
The Devonshire Regiment.
The Gloucester Regiment.
The Liverpool Regiment.

Rumours of war and warlike preparation on the part of the Boers were continually being circulated, and at daybreak on October 11th the Transvaal Boers crossed the frontier of Natal 18,000 strong with fourteen guns.

On October 12th, at 2 p.m., orders were received for the Regiment to prepare at once to go out as part of a flying column towards

Acton Holmes to check the advance of the Free State Boers, who were reported to be crossing the Biggarsberg by Vanreenen's Pass; and at 2 a.m. a force consisting of four regiments of cavalry, four batteries R.A., and three regiments of infantry (Liverpools, Gordons, and Devons) left Ladysmith, and after great delay reached Dewdrop at 9 a.m.

The cavalry having been sent on to gain touch, failed however to do so, and the column returned at once to Ladysmith. The information turned out to be incorrect.

On the return march the Regiment was joined by Captain W. B. Lafone and Lieutenants Field and Green, who had arrived from England.

On Sunday, October 15th, the Royal Irish Fusiliers, who had arrived about two days previously, marched out of the Tin Camp Ladysmith to entrain for Dundee, which place it was reported the Transvaal Boers were threatening; and on the same day the news was confirmed that the armoured train at Mafeking had been twice attacked.

It was said that our khaki uniform had

A REGIMENT OF THE LINE

completely nonplussed the Boers, and that they had expected to meet us coming on in red, as in the days gone by, and that they were consequently rather surprised and annoyed.

The Liverpool Regiment, 18th Hussars, and one battery left Ladysmith by road for Colenso on October 18th, the Manchester Regiment, the Devons, and Natal mounted troops covering their march from the direction of Vanreenen's Pass. Refugees continually coming through into Ladysmith from Acton Holmes during the day, reported fighting going on between Boers and Natal Carbineers.

On its return to Ladysmith the same day, the Regiment moved from the Tin Town Camp and encamped on the football ground under the convent hill, and towards sunset the whole army marched out of Ladysmith into strategical positions outside the town. The Regiment at this time was reserve battalion.

On October 19th the Boers cut the telegraph wire between Dundee and Ladysmith, and captured near Elandslaagte Station a train containing forty tons of flour consigned to the force at Dundee, and the following morning the Devons, Gordons, one battery, 5th Lancers, and some Colonial mounted infantry, moved out towards Modder Station on the Ladysmith-Newcastle road.

At about 11 a.m. news was received that a fierce battle was being fought at Dundee, and that a large force of Free State Boers was advancing towards Ladysmith from Bester's Station, having crossed the Vanreenen's Pass. The column was halted about four miles out of Ladysmith, and three companies of the Devons under Captain Travers were sent to hold Pepworth Hill on the flank threatened by the Free State Boers. But at 4 p.m. Sir George White came out and joined the force, and he ordered the column back into Ladysmith.

He gave an account of the fighting at Dundee, which he had just received. Dundee Camp was aroused in the morning by shells being pitched into its midst. The artillery came into action, and the 60th Rifles and Dublin Fusiliers were then sent to capture the position, which was occupied by 4000 Boers.

This was gallantly carried. Another column of Boers was then turned on to, and at 1.30 p.m. the enemy broke. Major-General Penn-Symons was mortally wounded, and Major-General Yule had taken over command at Dundee.

By next day a detachment of Boers had reached the neighbourhood of Modder Station and had taken up a position near Elandslaagte.

This detachment consisted of some 650 Boers, with two guns, under the leadership of General Koch, who was charged with the task of cutting off the retreat of the forces at Glencoe and Dundee, and who had been sent forward for that purpose. General Koch had at the same time practically joined hands with the Free State Boers, who were in the neighbourhood of Bester's Station on the Ladysmith-Harrismith line.

In order to reoccupy Elandslaagte and to secure General Yule's line of retreat, Sir George White ordered out a force consisting of infantry, cavalry, and artillery, of which four companies of the Regiment formed a part, under the command of General French.

These companies went out in the morning by train under Major Curry, and detrained near Modder Station.

One company and a Maxim gun under Captain Jacson and a squadron 5th Lancers were sent at 11 a.m. by road to Pepworth Hill to guard the left flank of General French's force against the Free State Army, which might seriously threaten General French's communications with Ladysmith.

At 1 p.m. further reinforcements were sent out to General French, and the three remaining companies of the Regiment were ordered to proceed by train to Modder Station to join the wing under Major Curry. The seven companies were then under the command of Major Park.

The Boers occupied two cones of some low hills overlooking Elandslaagte railway station. General French's artillery came into action on some high ground 4400 yards distant from the Boer position, and between the two forces was an open undulating plain affording little or no cover, and across which the attack had to be delivered.

The Gordon Highlanders and Manchesters

A REGIMENT OF THE LINE 15

were to attack round the Boers' left flank, whilst the Devons were to make a frontal attack.

From the nature of the position which they had taken up, no commanding positions affording flanking fire and protection to their flanks were obtainable by the Boers. These were open and could be easily threatened by the cavalry and the mounted infantry.

The Boers had two guns in position on one of the two cones, and with these guns they did good execution, knocking over a limber of one of French's batteries at the second shot, and practically before his guns came into action.

General French's force, now considerably augmented, marched off at 2.30 p.m. The 1st Devon Regiment was formed in company column at fifty paces as a reserve to the Manchester Regiment. After proceeding about a mile heavy firing was heard on the right front, direction was changed half-right, and the Regiment was then ordered to form for attack on the left of the Manchesters, and to take up a front of 500 yards.

Three companies were placed in the firing-line and supports under Major Park, and four companies in reserve under Major Curry. At about 3.15 p.m. the firing-line reached the top of a low hill, and came in sight of the enemy's position distant about 4400 yards. Here a halt of a quarter of an hour was made, and at 3.30 p.m. orders were received by the Regiment to make a frontal attack on the position, to advance to within effective rifle range, and to then hold on till a flank attack by the Manchesters and Gordons came in on the right. The ground between the Regiment and the position sloped slightly up to the foot of the low rocky hills, on which the enemy was posted. There was no cover of any kind, except a few ant-heaps, in the first half of the distance.

The firing-line advanced keeping intervals and covering a front of about 600 yards, the centre being directed on to a conical hill at the back of the enemy's camp. The reserve followed in column of companies, in single rank, at fifty paces distance between companies. The enemy's guns opened on the Regiment at once with shrapnel, but most of the shells went high, only one striking the reserve companies.

A steady advance to about 1200 to 1300 yards from the position was made, when, the rifle fire becoming rather heavy, fire was opened by section volleys. The light was bad, and it was very difficult to see the enemy or estimate the distances. In a few minutes the supports reinforced, and the firing-line then pushed on to the foot of the slope, and established itself in a shallow ditch 800 to 900 yards from the position. Here it held on, firing sectional volleys, till the flank attack appeared on the hill, apparently about 500 yards from the position.

An advance by companies from the right was then ordered, and, the reserve reinforcing, a further 200 yards was gained. Some bugling and shouting was then heard on the hill. A rush to 350 yards was now made, and, after a short pause to allow the men to get breath, bayonets were fixed and the position charged, four companies assaulting the detached hill on the left, the remaining three companies assaulting the hill on which the enemy's guns were. F and G Companies were the first to reach and take possession of the guns, the Gordon Highlanders coming up on the right shortly afterwards. The companies then moved on down the reverse slope and opened fire on the retiring enemy. On the detached hill only five of the enemy were found alive, and they showed a white flag as the hill was charged.

The Regiment was then re-formed, and held the detached hill during the night.

During the three hours it was under fire, the battalion kept line and intervals carefully throughout, and adjusted sights and fired as steadily as if on parade. It is to the perfect steadiness of the men and the absence of all crowding that the very small losses from the enemy's fire, which at all times was heavy, can be attributed.

The battalion's losses were :—

Captain W. B. Lafone, slightly wounded.

2nd Lieutenants Gunning, Hailey, and Green, severely wounded.

Twenty-nine non-commissioned officers and men wounded.

Parties of men were busy during the night

collecting the Boer wounded and taking them down to the laager. Among them was General Koch, who was badly hit in several places. He died of his wounds a few days afterwards in Ladysmith.

The losses of the Boers were estimated at 62 killed, 150 wounded, and 184 prisoners.

The force was moved back into Ladysmith early on the 22nd morning, the infantry by rail, and cavalry by road. The company of the Regiment and Maxim gun, which had been on Pepworth Hill during the day and the following night, got back to camp the same afternoon.

The 23rd was given up to rejoicings and congratulations over the victory, and the two Boer flags which were captured were displayed outside the officers' mess tent.

The Free State Army had by now come across to the east, and were in the neighbourhood of Modder Station, and on October 24th a column was again ordered out with the object of assisting General Yule's force in from Dundee.

This column consisted of the 5th Lancers,

19th Hussars, Natal Carbineers, Border Mounted Rifles, Imperial Light Horse, Devons, Liverpools, Gloucesters, 60th Rifles, and twenty guns, in all about 5500 men.

The enemy was found posted on Tinta Inyoni Mountain, on the summit of which they brought a gun into action and fired on to the head of Sir G. White's force, which was in column of route on the road, but without doing any damage. The action began at 8.30 a.m.

At the commencement of the action the battalion was in reserve, and was ordered to extend and lie down at the foot of the first slope facing the enemy's position, and some 300 yards north-west of the railway line, sending scouts to the crest of the ridge to watch the front. Four companies were shortly afterwards ordered to advance in attack formation, forming their own supports, and to place themselves on the left of the Gloucester Regiment, which was in front of the Regiment at the time. The Regiment was then on the extreme left of the firing-line. The four companies of the reserve worked round under cover to a small nullah about 300 yards on the left and then advanced up it. The firing-line advanced, under slight rifle fire, across a rocky plateau till they gained a small ridge overlooking the front, and opened fire by section volleys on to a ridge about 800 yards in front, from which a rather heavy fire was coming.

The Maxim gun under Lieutenant Price-Dent came into action in rear of the left of the line and fired at the enemy to the left front.

The enemy's fire from this ridge was soon silenced, and from that time the only objective the line had was a few scattered Boers and their horses on the rear slope of the high hill to the left front, some 2000 yards distant.

The reserve was deployed into two lines of double companies on and below a small ridge of rocks some 250 yards in rear of the firing-line. At about 2 p.m. the retirement commenced, and the battalion gradually followed the Liverpool Regiment and became rear-guard. Ladysmith was reached about 3.30 p.m., after a sixteen-mile march in torrents of rain.

The casualties of the battalion during the day were :—

1 private killed.[1]

25 privates wounded, none dangerously.

This action was known as the action of Reitfontein.

On October 26th General Yule's force marched into Ladysmith. They had had a bad time, having marched in drenching rain, day and night, from Sunday till Wednesday. The garrison of Ladysmith gave them food on arrival, the Regiment supplying the Dublin Fusiliers (officers and men) with refreshments.

On October 27th it was reported that the Boers were nearing Ladysmith and attempting to surround the place, and a large force was ordered out by Sir George White to reconnoitre.

This reconnaissance was under the command of Colonel Ian Hamilton, and his column consisted of three cavalry regiments, three batteries, and four infantry battalions, to

---

[1] This private, the first man of the Regiment killed in the war, was Private Winsor. He was shot dead through the heart by a stray bullet.

A REGIMENT OF THE LINE

which was added later one infantry battalion and one battery.

Having advanced beyond the Nek between Lombards Kop and Bulwana, and having crossed the Modder Spruit on the Helpmakaar road, the Regiment was sent on outpost duty to the left front, whilst the main body of the force halted on the bank of the stream.

From the outpost line large bodies of the enemy were observed advancing over Long Hill. Boers were also seen very busy on the kopjes south of Long Hill, entrenching.

At 8 p.m. orders were received from the officer commanding the column, in which it was explained that the force was to make a night march and attack, the infantry to advance at 2 a.m.

The Boer position as seen by the Regiment on the outpost line was some three miles in length, and the point of attack was to be the extreme left of their position, viz. Farquhar's Farm.

In the opinion of some the attack would have succeeded and the evil days of the siege put back; in the opinion of others the attack could not possibly have succeeded on account of the length of the Boer position, which they had had time to strengthen and entrench, and which had not been definitely reconnoitred.

At midnight fresh orders were received from Sir George White in Ladysmith. The whole force was ordered to retire and to proceed back at once into their positions in and about the town.

It was reported that the Boers were in great numbers, some 17,000 under Joubert, and that they had their big guns with them.

The Regiment commenced their retirement as rearguard to the force at 4 a.m., and reached camp at 6.30 a.m. on October 28th.

October 29th was a Sunday, and except for rumours, which were prolific, a quiet day was spent.

The Boers were reported to be entrenching themselves a mile and a half out on the Dundee road, and at the same time the Ladysmith defences were being prepared, and blasting operations were being carried out for the construction of military roads.

The battle of Farquhar's Farm was fought on October 30th, 1899.

The whole army was ordered out at 3 a.m.

The battalion formed part of the reserve brigade under Colonel Ian Hamilton. This reserve brigade took up a position under Limit Hill, and facing Pepworth Hill from the south.

The plan of the day was to have been as follows, had everything gone as it was proposed :—

Five regiments of infantry, all the mounted troops, and four batteries of artillery were to move round the enemy's left up the Helpmakaar road towards Farquhar's Farm (the direction of the proposed night attack on the night 27th-28th) to attack and drive in his left.

Two regiments of infantry with one mountain battery were to move off to the left of the British position to hold the enemy's right (which comprised the whole of the Free State Army), and prevent him from getting into Ladysmith.

The main attack was to be made in the centre by Colonel Ian Hamilton's Brigade by an assault on Pepworth Hill, where the Boer big guns were located, and which was the key of the position.

The above was the plan ; the result and the way in which it was carried out is told in a few words.

The two infantry battalions and mountain battery, detailed to guard the left flank, knocked up against the Free State Army under Cronje (which was seen in the forenoon by the main body of General White's force, coming over Walker's Hoek) on what is known now as Surprise Hill, and which place is situated a little above and nearer Ladysmith than Nicholson's Nek. Cronje attacked them in the dark, scattered the gun mules which stampeded, and after some hours of hard fighting captured the lot.

The force on the right, under Sir George White's personal command, ran prematurely into Joubert's Transvaal Army, which had advanced from its previous and partly reconnoitred position, and which had formed up ready to receive them in a position somewhat nearer Ladysmith. It received a very heavy cross fire from big guns,

A REGIMENT OF THE LINE 27

field guns, machine guns, and musketry, and was put to confusion, the artillery and the cavalry having some difficulty in extricating themselves. General White took the Manchester Regiment and the Gordon Highlanders from Hamilton's Brigade to cover the retirement, and his force came back into Ladysmith fired into with wonderful accuracy, at a range of about 7000 yards, by the big gun on Pepworth. Of the remainder of Hamilton's Brigade, the Rifle Brigade (which had only arrived in Ladysmith that day) and a half battalion Devon Regiment were told off to bring up the rear, whilst the other half battalion of the Devons was left on Limit Hill, two miles outside Ladysmith, to act as a covering force.

The Naval Brigade under Lambton arrived at Limit Hill with three naval 12-pounders just as the retirement was taking place, and they were at once ordered back into the town. They returned without coming into action. As they were retiring down the road past the Piggery by the Orange Free State Junction Station, a well-aimed shell from

Pepworth Hill upset one of their guns, killing some of the ox-team and a gunner who was being carried back wounded in an ambulance.

The half battalion of the regiment under Major Curry was ordered to take up a defensive position on Limit Hill and to stay there for the night.

The Boer force was within 1000 yards, and it was thought probable that they would follow up their defeated foe. Their patrols were continually coming to within 300–500 yards of the Devons' outpost line.

As the half battalion was well covered from view, it was deemed expedient and prudent not to expose their position and weakness by firing, but rather by lying quiet to trust to the Boer imagination, allowing them to think there was a larger force in position at Limit Hill than there really was. This plan was eminently successful, for except for Boer patrols the position was not threatened.

Orders were received by this half battalion at 9 a.m. on November 2nd to retire on to Ladysmith. The defenders of Ladysmith being unaware of the fact that any of their own troops were in front of them, and mis-

A REGIMENT OF THE LINE

taking friend for foe, got down on their knees to fire as the companies of the Devons appeared in sight.

The half battalion which had retired with the rest of the force into Ladysmith on October 30th received orders at 10 a.m. on the 31st to strike camp, move off and form part of the garrison of section "A" of the defences of Ladysmith, under the command of Colonel W. G. Knox, c.b. The second half battalion followed them.

CHAPTER II

SIEGE OF LADYSMITH

1899-1900

THE siege of Ladysmith had now commenced; communication to the south was interrupted on November 2nd, and on the same day the Boers had their guns in action on Bulwana Mountain and were shelling the works and town freely.

The perimeter of Ladysmith was divided into four sections, A, B, C, D, under Colonel W. G. Knox, General Howard, Colonel Hamilton, and Colonel Royston respectively. Section A extended from Devon Post to Cove Redoubt; on the west of this was section B, extending as far as Range Post on the Klip River. Section C included Maiden Castle, Wagon Hill, and Cæsar's Camp, whilst the plain between Cæsar's Camp and Devon Post was held by the Natal Volunteers under Colonel Royston.

The battalion was ordered to take up the two posts of Cemetery Hill and Helpmakaar Hill. These were the most eastern kopjes of the defences. They skirted the Helpmakaar road and were immediately under Bulwana and Gun Hill. These were distant only some five thousand yards, and dominated Devon Post.

The battalion was distributed: three companies on Helpmakaar Hill, two companies on Cemetery Hill, with three companies in reserve near the road and river-bed immediately beneath Cemetery Hill.

Devon Post received its first shells on the morning of the 3rd. These were aimed at the tents of the reserve companies, which were rather ostentatiously pitched on the plain by the river-bed under Cemetery Hill. The shells were fired from a high-velocity 3-inch gun on Bulwana. The tents were immediately moved closer under the hill, where they were out of sight from Bulwana. The Boer guns were then trained on to the working parties, and some fifty shells were burst in the works (just commenced and affording little cover) on Helpmakaar and Cemetery

Hill posts, but without doing much damage. After this, owing to shell fire, it was impossible to work except at night, or when Bulwana was obscured by fog. The fortifications and defences were, however, hastily pushed forward, and the platforms for the two large and ancient howitzers known as "Castor" and "Pollux" were soon completed.

Shortly after the commencement of the siege one of the few shells fired into Ladysmith which did any damage, burst amongst a party of Natal Carbineers on the road under Cemetery Hill, killing five men and seven horses.

On November 5th the Intombi Camp was formed, and all the wounded and most of the women and children, with a few of the able-bodied male civilian inhabitants of Ladysmith, were moved into the neutral camp.

On November 6th and 7th, with the exception of a shell or two, things were quiet on Devon Post, but on the evening of the 7th a furious bombardment began at four o'clock, the Boer guns all round firing into the town and at anything they could see moving. No damage was done.

A REGIMENT OF THE LINE

In addition to the works on Devon Post, which were manned by the Regiment, a half-company picquet was told off nightly. This picquet extended and lay down across the main road at the foot of the forward work. It mounted after dark and was relieved before daylight in the morning. Many will remember the spot where this picquet was posted as the most ill-chosen, inconvenient, and hard platform for a bed on a rainy night.

The nights of the 6th, 7th, and 8th were occupied in making the works stronger and building additional works.

On November 9th the Boers made their first attempt against Ladysmith. The attack commenced at 6 a.m. with heavy musketry fire directed on to the northern defences; and three hours later the attack developed on Helpmakaar Post and Cæsar's Camp. Shells came very thickly from two howitzers and three high-velocity Creusot guns into Devon Post. This lasted till about 2 p.m., when the action was concluded with a royal salute from the naval batteries and three hearty cheers, which, started by the Naval Brigade, were taken up all round the defences in honour of the birthday of H.R.H. the Prince of Wales. A curious ending to a battle.

During the action a well-directed shell from one of Christie's ancient howitzers, which were now located on Helpmakaar Hill, pitched with good effect into the middle of a large group of Boers who were entrenching themselves on a small rise of ground underneath Gun Hill.

Helpmakaar, which had always been a single-day post, was now turned into a three days' post, companies remaining in the fort for three days before being relieved.

On the 11th three companies of the Regiment were sent out under Captain Lafone to blow up a farm building under Bulwana, about one and half miles distant from Devon Post. After a long delay, owing to the blasting materials having been forgotten, the operation was successfully carried out, and the party returned with only some slight annoyance from the enemy's pompom and a few shots from a high-velocity gun stationed on Bulwana.

The Boer artillery on Bulwana and Gun Hill was well served, and their shooting was excellent. One morning they opened with a

40-pounder howitzer, known under the name of "Weary Willy," on to the main work at Devon Post, at a portion of the work occupied by "Walker's Hotchkiss Gun Detachment." About twelve consecutive shots pitched within a five yards' radius, and one crashed into and nearly breached the parapet, which was here about six feet thick and built of large stones.

The men worked on the 11th from dark till 1 a.m., when the works were practically completed and sufficiently strengthened to answer all purposes, although building was being carried on till the last day of the siege, and the men were still building at the actual moment when the relief cavalry were marching across the plain into Ladysmith.

The willingness and the cheery manner in which the men of the battalion worked at these defences are worthy of record. On pitch-dark nights in pouring rain the men, wet to the skin, covered with mud and filth, without a smoke, groping about in the dark to find a likely stone, carried on the work in silence; and when the word was passed along to knock off work, they "turned in" without a grumble into a wet bivouac. There was no complaining, and the men were never required by their officers to bring along the stones faster. The only noise that broke the stillness of the night was the incessant "click, click, click" of the picks at work loosening the stones, and the men, in spite of the conditions under which the work was being carried on, joked among themselves in an undertone.

Work was nightly carried on from dark till midnight and sometimes till 2 a.m., and the men turned out again to stand to arms at 3.30 a.m.

By the middle of November the works at Devon Post were from $4\frac{1}{2}$ to 10 feet high, from 8 to 10 feet thick at the top (the whole built roughly of stone), with the superior slope nearly flat, exterior slope about 1/1, interior slope nearly upright. The front work had a thickness at the bottom of about 18 feet, owing to the work being constructed on the slope of the hill.

Things passed quietly with intermittent shell fire till the afternoon of the 14th, when General Brocklehurst took out the Cavalry Brigade and two batteries of artillery, with the intention of turning the Boers off Rifleman's

IN THE TRENCHES, LADYSMITH

A REGIMENT OF THE LINE 37

Ridge. This they failed to do, and returned to their lines about 5 p.m. well peppered by the Boer big guns, one shell from the big gun on Pepworth pitching into the centre of the road just short of a battery of artillery which was coming back into Ladysmith, near the defences on the north-west front held by a detachment of the Dublin Fusiliers—an accurate shot, and the distance measured on the map 10,500 yards. Shortly afterwards the Naval Brigade in their turn did some good shooting, pitching a shell on to the muzzle of the big gun on Pepworth, and a few moments after this shot, another on to his parapet. Boers were afterwards seen carrying litters away from the work. This big gun never fired again during the siege, but the Boers patched him up and he lived to do good work for them against General Buller in his advance north to Lydenburg, and the Boers finally blew him up in front of the battalion near Waterval, in the Lydenburg district, when engaged with a column under General Walter Kitchener.

For the next few days nothing of consequence occurred beyond the usual shell fire, varied at intervals from day to night time. It rained in torrents most of the time, and the men were continually wet through. They however kept very fit, and there were very few in hospital.

An amusing incident occurred on the 17th. Good targets being scarce the Boers continually fired shell at any moving or stationary object they could catch sight of—sometimes at a single scout. They often fired their pompom at a range of about 5000 yards at the vultures feeding on the dead horses under Devon Post. On this day they sent three 40-lb. shells at an old man named Brown who contracted for the dead horses. Brown used to take these out into the open in full view of the Boers, to some flat ground under the Post, and there skin them at his leisure. The old man would take his load out once a day in a four-horsed cart. If he was seen by the Boers he would come back at a gallop pursued by Boer shells. This time he came back on three wheels, much to the amusement of Section A of the defences; the fourth wheel had come off and he was in too great a hurry to readjust it, and it was in consequence left behind. The old man was never hit.

On November 20th the Boers mounted some more guns on Bulwana and also on Umbrella Tree Hill, which lay in the Nek between Bulwana and Gun Hill. Colonel Knox ordered a dummy battery to be made at night on the further side of the Klip River and out in the open. Wooden imitation guns and imitation gunners were erected, and these were worked with a string by a gunner concealed in the bank of the river.

Captain Kincaid-Smith, with the two Maxim-Nordenfeldt guns captured at Elandslaagte, of which he was now in charge, was to open fire from Devon Post on to the Boer guns newly placed on Umbrella Tree Hill, and as he was perfectly concealed and fired smokeless powder, it was supposed that the Boers would imagine that the firing came from the new dummy battery just erected.

Kincaid-Smith began firing at about six o'clock on the following morning. He fired some five shells in perfect silence unanswered by the Boers. He was then suddenly located by them, and shells were hurled on to him from all sides and from all descriptions of guns. This continued for a quarter of an hour and then slackened off. The Boers burst their shrapnel better than usual, and in the evening just before dark one shrapnel got into a working party on Devon Post, killing one man and severely wounding another.

There was some heavy musketry fire during the night at a reconnaissance party sent out from Ladysmith towards Umbrella Tree Hill. The party had orders to disturb the Boers and draw their fire. This they very successfully accomplished. On the 22nd night another "disturbing party" was sent out under Captain Jacson, consisting of one company of the Regiment and a party of cavalry, to "stir up" the Boers on Flag Hill. It was pitch-dark, pouring with rain, and the ground was covered with boulders of rocks. The cavalry were obliged to leave their horses behind and proceed on foot in front of the infantry; so little was gained by the enterprise and no "stirring up" was effected.

Up to this date there had been very little news from the outside world, but now the Regiment was informed that General French had fought a successful engagement at Estcourt and had got in with the cavalry. They were also told that the garrison might expect to be relieved by the 13th December by one division which was coming up from Durban.

About November 22nd the news was received that the armoured train at Colenso had been attacked, derailed, and captured.

On the 23rd Kincaid-Smith received orders to proceed with one of his guns during the following night down to the river-bed near the dummy battery and open fire if the Boers fired at it in the morning. This they had done the previous day, much to every one's amusement. At daybreak he opened fire from the river-bed. After his second shot the Boers found him and made wonderful practice, bursting shrapnel all over him. No damage, however, was done as he was well dug into the bank. They continued their shelling for an hour, after which they turned their big guns on to Tunnel Hill for a short time. This hill was held by the Liverpool Regiment, who lost two killed and twelve wounded, of whom five died of their wounds next day.

The works on Devon Post and Cemetery Hill were strengthened during the next few nights until the front walls were from twelve to fifteen feet thick. Most of this work was carried on in heavy rain, which greatly added to the general discomfort of the men.

On November 28th the garrison was encouraged by the information that the Boers had been badly beaten near Estcourt, that 3000 of them had gone off (it was not reported where to!), and that General Clery was at Colenso.

On November 30th General Clery opened up signalling communication with Ladysmith by flashing his message with his searchlight at night on to the clouds. The message, which was in cipher, could be easily read by every one, but the garrison was unable to reply as they had no searchlight.

In the early days of December, in order to keep the men as far as possible in a condition for any eventualities, the Regiment evacuated their works twice a week at dusk and went for a march twice round the town. Starting at nightfall the works were regained about 10 p.m. The exercise was good for the men's limbs and the change of scene undoubtedly nourishment for their minds, but it is doubtful if it conduced to the health of the men, as during the march they were smothered in their own

A REGIMENT OF THE LINE 43

dust, and also in that kicked up by the artillery horses exercising at the same time and on the same roads. It certainly gave the men something to think about besides rocks and stones and building, and the walking stretched their legs.

On December 2nd Colonel Knox, desirous of carrying on the work of building in the daytime as well as by night, ordered some canvas screens to be put up in the Post, behind which the men could work concealed from view. But although stained the colour of the surroundings, the screens were seen at once by the Boers, and the battalion was much troubled by a new gun stationed near Pepworth Hill, which opened fire shortly after they were erected. One shell from this howitzer topping the hill pitched within a yard of the guard tent underneath, which was full of men. No damage was done, however, beyond scattering the ammunition boxes and covering the men with mud. The screens were then taken down, and on the disappearance of the noxious objects the firing ceased, and the Boers appeared pacified. At 10 p.m., whilst the Regiment was at work building on Cemetery Hill, an order came to parade at once and march to a rendezvous down in the town in Lyle Street. It was given out "for operations near Limit Hill." On reaching the rendezvous it was learnt that the force consisted of two brigades of infantry, some batteries, and all the mounted troops. After half an hour's wait, a staff officer rode up to say that the operations were cancelled.

About this time the siege newspaper, the *Ladysmith Lyre*, came into existence. There were only four issues, on account of want of paper.

Shelling continued daily with but little or no result. The Boers were apparently much incensed with the Town Hall, upon which the Geneva red cross flag was flying, and which was being used as a hospital, for they continually fired at it till the flag was taken down early in December, when they scarcely ever fired at it again.

On December 7th General Hunter made his sortie to Gun Hill. The secret was well kept. In the evening, at dark, the battalion was sent to Abattis Hill with orders to entrench, the scheme ostensibly being that a

TOWN HALL, LADYSMITH, CLOCK-TOWER DAMAGED BY SHELL FIRE

force was to go out and stir up the Boers round Pepworth Hill whilst the Regiment threatened to attack the Boers on the other flank.

At 11 p.m. a letter was received telling the officer commanding the Devon Regiment to meet General Hunter under Devon Post at 11.30 p.m. Shortly after this hour a force of Colonial mounted infantry, with General Hunter at their head, passed the post to assault Gun Hill. This they found but sparsely guarded, and, dispersing the small picquet, they succeeded in blowing up the two big guns and a Maxim located there. The Regiment remained out till the operation was over. It had been placed in this position on Abattis Hill to act as a flank guard, with the object of preventing the Boers attacking from the left round General Hunter's rear, which was very open, and to act as a support upon which General Hunter could fall back in case his surprise failed and he was driven in.

This successful operation was accomplished with the loss of seven men wounded.

The operation that followed was not, however, so successful. Colonel Knox reported that his mounted troops had gone out eight miles up the Newcastle road past Limit Hill, and had not met or seen a single Boer. He suggested that the Cavalry Brigade should go out and capture and burn the Boer stores at Elandslaagte Station. They proceeded to carry out the suggestion, starting at 7 a.m., but they fell in with a large force of Boers under Pepworth Hill who had been in their laagers when the reconnaissance was made and had thus escaped detection. They came under heavy musketry fire as well as shell fire, and retired back to Ladysmith with a loss of three killed and fifteen wounded.

On December 10th an attack on Devon Post was expected, and precautions taken accordingly. The attack, however, did not come off.

On the night of December 10th the Rifle Brigade made a sortie and blew up a Boer big gun on Surprise Hill. This attack was admirably planned and carried out, but the losses sustained by the Rifle Brigade were heavy, being fourteen killed and fifty wounded out of the five companies employed. The Boers attacked them as they were retiring; there was a good

A REGIMENT OF THE LINE

deal of indiscriminate firing, and the bayonet was freely used. The Boers lost considerably, partly in the general mix-up, from their own fire, and partly owing to the close-quarter combat with the Rifle Brigade.

The Regiment, with other troops, was ordered out with all baggage on the night of the 12th, the rendezvous being the iron bridge on the Vanreenen's Pass road. On arrival there the order was received to go home. This was supposed to be a rehearsal for a sortie. On December 13th General Buller's guns were heard for the first time due south from Ladysmith, and at 8 p.m. the Regiment and transport were inspected by Colonel Knox to see if everything was complete and in readiness to move out, and on the 14th the Regiment was placed with other troops in a flying column formed under the personal command of Sir George White.

It was expected by all that General Buller would relieve the Ladysmith garrison on December 15th.

The following day, December 15th, a very heavy cannonade commenced at 6 a.m. in the direction of Colenso; and at 7 a.m. a heliograph message was sent into Ladysmith which told the garrison that "the Boers are suffering terribly from our thirty guns and 23,000 men." The cannonade ceased at about 1 p.m.

This day the meat ration was reduced to 9 oz. per man, but $1\frac{1}{4}$ lb. of bread per man was still being issued.

December 16th being Dingaan's Day, the garrison of Ladysmith was treated to heavy shell fire at daybreak.

On December 17th the Regiment and the Gordon Highlanders were told off as reserve battalions under the immediate orders of Sir George White.

It was officially given out that Sir R. Buller had been unable to make good his advance at Colenso, and that the garrison must be prepared to hold on for another two weeks. The orders publishing this news stated that the "Lieutenant-General regrets to have to announce that the Lieutenant-General Commanding-in-Chief in South Africa failed to make good his first attack on Colenso; reinforcements will therefore not arrive as early as expected."

On the evening of December 18th the Regi-

A REGIMENT OF THE LINE

ment gave over the good works they had completed on Devon Post and Cemetery Hill to the Liverpool Regiment, and moved into the latter's camp at Tunnel Hill, or, as it was otherwise known, Railway Cutting Camp.

Helpmakaar Hill, on account of being so exposed, had, at the commencement of the siege, been considered indefensible and untenable.

Under the vigorous superintendence of Colonel Knox, the commandant of the section who planned the defences, the works on this hill had by now been almost completed by the officers and men of the Battalion.

The defences were as complete as possible—flanking works, covered ways, splinter and shell-proof covers were dug or erected, and the main trenches had been turned into defensible barracks with head cover to keep off the rain.

It was possible to proceed from the reserve under Cemetery Hill up to and round the front and main works, and round the other side of the hill back to the reserve again, without once coming into view from the Boer positions on Gun Hill, Bulwana, or elsewhere, a six-feet covering wall having been built for this purpose. It was thus possible to send reinforcements to any part of the works without exposure to fire or view.

During the siege this post was never attacked or seriously threatened.

The Regiment, being now in the general reserve, was ordered to be ready to jump into mule wagons, and be carted at a gallop to any place where they might be required, at any moment, and on the 20th the manœuvre was put into execution.

It was not altogether a success.

At dusk the Regiment proceeded to the railway station and the men were duly loaded up in the wagons. A start was then made, but as the second wagon nearly took the whole station with it in its endeavours to negotiate the first corner of the galvanized iron goods shed, no great speed was effected, for this wagon and the demolished corner of the shed blocked all further egress from the station till the road was cleared. Shortly afterwards the wagons, at last let loose, came into contact with the two city filth carts, the "Powerful"

A REGIMENT OF THE LINE

and "Terrible," which were parading about the streets on their own. These exceedingly powerful ironclads completed the defeat of the mule wagons, upset finally their order of going, and the retirement was effected in detachments. The manœuvre was never repeated.

Wonderful tales and reports were continually being circulated from day to day. On one day there would perhaps be no news of any value, followed on the next day by the most woeful tidings; but on the third day, as if ashamed of themselves for furnishing such bad news the previous day, the tale-bearers would turn the winter of its discontent into the most glorious summer, by sending forth to the garrison shaves bubbling over with pleasing items.

On the evening of the 21st a heliograph message was received from the 2nd Battalion, which was with Sir Redvers Buller, stating that at the Colenso fight on the 15th December Colonel Bullock, Major Walter, and Lieutenant Smyth-Osbourne had been taken prisoners, and Captains Goodwyn, Vigors, and Radcliffe and Lieutenants Gardiner and Storey wounded.

After standing to arms daily at 4.15 a.m.

till daylight, the Regiment was employed in building long stone traverses, behind which the men were to live, and this work was carried on again in the evening after dark by the light of candles. The dimensions of the traverses were sixty yards long, eight feet high, six feet (of stonework) thick at the top, and nine feet of stonework at the base, the earth from a ditch in front being thrown up at an angle of 1/1. They had a topping of sandbags, with intervals for air passage; and a tent, stretched lengthways from the top down to ground, afforded the men shelter and accommodation.

On December 22nd a serious catastrophe happened to a party of the Gloucester Regiment, who were quartered in a small traverse near those occupied by the Regiment. A shell caught the whole party of twelve men as they were sitting away from the cover of the traverse. Five were killed, four died of their wounds almost immediately, and three were severely wounded.

A man with a telescope was now placed on the look-out, with orders to blow a whistle if he saw the big gun on Bulwana turned towards

A REGIMENT OF THE LINE

the lines when firing; and as the shell took about thirty seconds from the time of the discharge to reach its mark, the warning gave the men time to get under cover.

There were frequently some very amusing incidents when the look-out man blew his whistle. One morning whilst the business at the orderly-room was being conducted, and a culprit being told off, the whistle gave warning that the gun on Bulwana had fired, and in the direction of Tunnel Hill. As all could not get inside the orderly-room shelter, which was merely a hole dug into the side of the hill, there was a general scuttle and *sauve qui peut*. One officer, trying to get into the orderly-room from outside, ran into another who was escaping from it to get into the first traverse, and each tumbled over the other. The Quartermaster, trying to crawl on his hands and knees under the tenting of the second traverse, got blocked out, and at the same time shut out another officer flying for safety. At the same moment a man jumped from above on the Quartermaster's back, and he, fancying that it was the shell and that his end had come, gave himself up for lost. All, however, ended happily for the immediate neighbourhood, for the look-out man had made a mistake, and the shell, instead of arriving at Tunnel Hill, crashed into the town.

All these incidents and accidents, individually very serious at the time, were always amusing in the telling as soon as the tyranny was overpast, and, resulting in a hearty laugh, helped to relieve the strain.

The London *Gazette* of October 9th was signalled into Ladysmith by the 2nd Battalion. This stated: "Major Park to be Lieutenant-Colonel; Davies, 2nd-in-Command; Ellicombe, Major; Radcliffe, Captain."

A list of prices at this time in Ladysmith at the public auction is of interest:—

Eggs per dozen, 11s. 6d.
Small vegetable marrow, 1s. 6d.
Twelve small carrots, 2s. 6d.
Small water melon (worth 1d.), 6s. 6d.
Condensed milk per tin, 5s. 6d.
Fifty-two small potatoes, £1 10s.
Chickens, each, 8s.
Ducks, 13s. 6d.
Dutch butter in tins, 6s. 6d. per lb.
½d. Manilla cigars, 1s.

There was no English smoking tobacco obtainable, and one bottle of whisky changed hands at £5 10s.

December 25th, Christmas Day.

"Hark, the herald angels sing!" was forcibly brought to notice by the whistling of shells passing overhead at daylight. No Divine Service was therefore held. The garrison received the following message from Her Majesty the Queen: "I wish you and all my brave soldiers and sailors a happy Christmas. God protect and bless you all.—V.R.I." In the evening there was a soldiers' sing-song in the lines, which was finished off by three most hearty cheers for Her Majesty. Christmas Day completed the eighth week of the siege.

The losses which the 2nd Battalion sustained at Colenso were heliographed into Ladysmith. These were 15 N.C.O.'s and 10 men killed, 72 wounded, and 33 taken prisoners. This was in addition to the officers wounded and taken prisoners already mentioned.

On December 27th, shortly after breakfast, a shell from the big gun from Bulwana pitched and burst in the officers' mess shelter, where fourteen officers had taken cover on the whistle being blown. Lieutenant A. F. Dalzel was killed and the following were wounded :—

Lieutenant P. H. Price-Dent, dangerously in the head.
Lieutenant Caffin, dangerously in arm and shoulder.
Lieutenant Byrne, slightly.
Lieutenant Tringham, slightly.
Lieutenant Kane, slightly.
Lieutenant Scafe, slightly.
Lieutenant Twiss, slightly.
Lieutenant Blunt, slightly.
Captain Lafone, slightly.
Private Laycock, mess waiter, slightly.

The wounded were taken into the Railway Cutting and there cared for. They were then sent down to hospital in a church in the town. Lieutenant Dalzel was buried that night in the cemetery after dark during a heavy thunderstorm and in torrents of rain.

The men had a bad experience on the night of the 29th. The rain flooded their bivouacs, and the morning found blankets and clothes floating about in the water in the trenches.

AFTER A WET NIGHT IN THE TRAVERSES, LADYSMITH

A REGIMENT OF THE LINE 57

Later on, however, the weather cleared, the sun came out, and everything was soon dried.

At the latter end of December marksmen were sent out daily to the hill-tops some 1000 yards in front of the line of forts to act as countersnipers to the Boers, who continually fired at the grazing guards. One man was hit twice in one day by a Boer sniper, but only slightly wounded. It would appear from a letter written by a Boer that these marksmen made it very uncomfortable for the Boer snipers. In the letter, which was afterwards published in a Boer newspaper, the correspondent, writing to a friend in Pretoria, said: "I and my two comrades went out this morning to fire into the English position. We had only just got to our hiding-place when one of my comrades was shot dead; shortly after, my other comrade was badly wounded, and I lay down and hid the whole day till dark, when I got back to the laager." This would go to prove that, comparing him with the Boer, the British infantry soldier is not such a duffer with his weapon as some of those in authority were in the habit of asserting.

There was a good deal of musketry fire

whilst the scouts were out, and it was supposed that shots were being exchanged with the Boer snipers; but when the marksmen, who were posted on the hills near the Orange Free State Junction Station and just above the abandoned piggery, came back with portions of the carcasses of pigs, it was evident that all the firing had not been at Transvaal Boers.

Lieutenant Price-Dent died at 6 a.m. on the 31st December in the Intombi Hospital. It was found that a piece of shell had penetrated his brain and lodged there. He was buried in the Intombi cemetery.

Up to the end of December things had been going fairly well with the besieged. The Regiment had had plenty of hard work to keep them fit, although they had been exposed to the elements and had had to rough it considerably. But nothing in the way of disease had troubled them. With the advent of January, however, whether it was from want of exercise or from the surroundings of their new camp, disease in the form of fever and dysentery became rife. They had been situated formerly for the most part on a well-

A REGIMENT OF THE LINE

drained kopje, whereas now they were down on the flat, and in a position that was not altogether healthy. There were no longer any comforts in the shape of tobacco, etc., and the news given to them from the outside world in the place of food was of so poor a quality that the men's minds as well as their bodies were becoming affected.

The Regiment kept heart under the depressing circumstances in a wonderful manner, and when Sir Redvers Buller kept putting off his arrival from day to day and week to week, the news that he was coming at last was generally received with a smile as if it was rather a joke.

The Boers were very busy on New Year's Day, 1900. It was supposed that a number of excursion trains filled with the youth and beauty of the Transvaal had arrived, and consequently the young Boer blood was all for showing off. The big gun on Bulwana threw in the aggregate during the day $1\frac{1}{2}$ tons of iron into the town, with the result that two men were killed. There was likewise a good deal of sniping, chiefly at the Indian "grass cuts."

One shell thrown into Ladysmith on New Year's Day had engraved on it " Compliments of the season," and contained a bursting charge of liquorice in the place of melinite, and a paper on which was written :—

"Good morning Mr. Franchise, don't be so cowardly to stay in holes, ye brave hero.

"Your faithfully,

"Small Long Tom."

Another blind shell picked up was full of sweetmeats.

Messages of good wishes to the garrison were received from Her Majesty, from Sir Redvers Buller, and from the soldiers, sailors, and civilians of Hong Kong.

Sir George White came round to see the Regiment in the evening, and informed the officers that Sir Redvers Buller would make no move for a fortnight. This was definite news, at any rate.

At dawn on January 3rd most of the naval guns fired off a large amount of shell, and there was considerable guessing amongst the uninitiated as to what was or were the targets. Shells fell at the foot of Bulwana, near the searchlight on the top, and also near the big gun. It was afterwards learnt that all the shells were meant for one particular spot on Bulwana, viz. the big gun.

On occasions it was the duty of the Regiment to send one company to dismount the 4·7 gun known as "Lady Anne" and place it on carts preparatory to its being shifted elsewhere. This was easily accomplished at the commencement of the siege in one night by 100 men. At the end of the siege, however, owing to the weakness of the men, the task was never completed under two nights, and then by 200 men.

About this time one company of the Regiment was ordered down to the railway station as a station and bridge guard. This was a three-days' post, and was much appreciated, as the men, being quite concealed amongst trees, had more freedom, and the officer in command had a railway carriage to sleep in.

On January 5th the following moves took place, and as the position of companies is important, they are given in full.

Three companies proceeded under Major Curry to Observation Hill to relieve the companies of the 60th Rifles ordered to Cæsar's Camp. One company was ordered to the railway station as bridge guard. A half company was sent to form the Bell's Spruit picquet, the other half remaining at the Railway Cutting. In the early hours of January 6th three fresh companies relieved those on Observation Hill, the latter returning to the Railway Cutting ; the two companies at the railway bridge and at Bell's Spruit stood fast in their positions of the previous day.

The Boer attack of January 6th on the positions round Ladysmith commenced on Wagon Hill at about 2.45 a.m., and the Boers were not finally repulsed till after dark on the evening of the same day.

As the great attack has been so ably described by various authors, it will suffice here to give a rough outline of what took place on Cæsar's Camp and Wagon Hill prior to the companies of the Regiment reaching the latter place.

The Boers attacked Wagon Hill at about 2.45 a.m., and amidst a good deal of confusion on the top, where a 4·7 gun was in the act of being mounted, gained possession of the front

THE RAILWAY BRIDGE, WITH CÆSAR'S CAMP IN DISTANCE, LADYSMITH

A REGIMENT OF THE LINE 63

crest. Their attempt to take Wagon Hill itself failed. Reinforcements consisting of two companies Gordon Highlanders and three squadrons of I.L.H. were sent to assist the 60th Rifles, the men of the I.L.H., and the detachment of Sappers already engaged with the Boers.

An hour later the attack on Cæsar's Camp developed. The Manchesters were prepared for them, and one company Gordon Highlanders was sent to reinforce. The Boers, unable to advance against the front crest of Cæsar's Camp, attempted to turn the flank of the Manchesters along the northern slopes. This attempt was foiled by the advance of the one company Gordon Highlanders, assisted by the 53rd Battery which had come into action on the plain below. The Rifle Brigade reinforced Cæsar's Camp at about 7 a.m., and two more companies of the Gordons were sent there at about 2 p.m. By 10 a.m. the Boers had been pushed back off Cæsar's Camp, and Wagon Hill was reported nearly clear.

Wagon Hill was further reinforced by the 18th Hussars at 10 a.m.

At 1 p.m. the Boers, who had always hung

on to their crest line, again attempted to rush Wagon Hill point, and though they gained a temporary advantage failed to establish themselves.

Sir George White ordered that the hill should be cleared of Boers at all costs before nightfall, and he sent the 5th Lancers and 19th Hussars to support the troops already at Wagon Hill, and at the same time three companies of the Devons were ordered to proceed there with all dispatch.

At 10 a.m. the three companies of the Devons, which were in camp, commanded respectively by Captain W. B. Lafone, Lieutenant Masterson with Lieutenant Walker, and Lieutenant Field, the whole commanded by Lieutenant-Colonel Park, had been ordered to proceed to the camp near Iron Bridge vacated that morning by the Gordon Highlanders, to be ready as a reserve if wanted.

At about 3.30 p.m. these three companies received orders to proceed at once to Wagon Hill to reinforce Colonel Ian Hamilton's command and to push on, as help was urgently required. The Adjutant, Captain H. S. L. Ravenshaw, was sent back to camp to order rations and water to be sent out. Wagon Hill was reached at 4.45 p.m., and it was then ascertained that the 5th Lancers and 19th Hussars had already been merged into the firing line, and that a party of forty or fifty Boers were still in possession of the hill some 100 yards in front of the ridge held by the Imperial Light Horse, and directly in front of where the three companies were then halted under cover, that these Boers had been holding on all day there and inflicting great loss, and that our troops had been unable to dislodge them. Colonel Park was asked if he could turn them out by rushing them with the bayonet. He answered, "We will try." After the three companies had been formed up in column with bayonets fixed and magazines charged, Colonel Park gave the order to advance at fifty paces interval in quick time, and when the top of the ridge was reached to charge the position occupied by the Boers.

The charge took place in a blinding hailstorm, a time well chosen, as the hail was beating into the faces of the Boers. The men, before reaching the place where they formed up for the charge, were wet through, and had put on their warm coats which they had carried strapped on to their belts.

When the storm was at its height, Colonel Park gave the order to charge. Lieutenant Field, who commanded the leading company, rushed forward up the slope, shouting, "Company, double charge!" He was immediately followed at a distance of about ten yards by Masterson's company, which was immediately followed by Lafone's. As they got to the top of the crest they came in view of the sangar of rocks held by the I.L.H. At the corner of this they had to change direction half right, and the moment they reached it came under fire from the Boers. There was necessarily some crowding at this corner, owing to the change of direction, and the fact that the companies in their eagerness had followed so soon the one behind the other. There was, however, no halting, no dwelling here. On they went to reach their goal, 130 yards away, over perfectly flat open ground, fired into at short range from right, left, and front. Three-parts of the way across Park directed the rear company more to the right, the position the Boers occupied being in a semicircle.

LIEUT.-COLONEL C. W. PARK

The enemy held on, firing most heavily, until the charging lines were within fifteen yards of them, and then ran down the slope and disappeared behind a ridge of rocks some forty yards ahead, beyond which the ground was dead and fell steeply away to the front. Almost before the men could be secured in the position they had won, bullets began to come in quickly from the right and left, and the cover of the rocks had to be sought as several men were hit. A few of the Boers who had been dislodged also crept back to the low ridge of rocks in front and began firing, and it was at this time that Captain Lafone and Lieutenant Field were hit. Lieutenant Walker, Somerset Light Infantry, and about thirty-five men were hit during the charge. Colonel Park was then the only officer left, the three companies being commanded by non-commissioned officers.

Lieutenant Walker was one of the last shot dead in the charge. He was shot through the head (as were most of the killed) within fifteen yards of the kopje held by the Boers.

Lieutenant Field rushed forward beyond this kopje and lay down in the open and commenced firing at the Boers at the crest just in front. He was very shortly afterwards shot through the head.

Captain Lafone was shot shortly before Lieutenant Field. He was in the act of firing at the time, taking aim, and was shot by a Boer lying in the grass some twenty-five yards away on his right rear. Before he was killed he had suggested to Lieutenant Masterton that some one should go back to the I.L.H. sangar to ask them to direct their fire on to some Boers on the left front; these were firing into the dead and wounded who had been hit during the charge and left out in the open.

Lieutenant Masterton at once volunteered, and started to run back over the 130 yards. He got most of the way across when he was hit in the legs by a bullet, but he continued his course, and being struck again fell, and was dragged behind cover by the I.L.H. He delivered his message.

The position won was held until the Boers retired under cover of darkness. The men were then placed in defensive positions, and picquets told off.

The wounded were subsequently cared for,

A REGIMENT OF THE LINE 69

and the dead left where they had fallen till daylight.

Colonel Park described the fire of the Boers as like the crackle of a piece of gorse in a blazing fire. Colour-Sergeant Palmer, who so greatly distinguished himself both during and after the charge, said the air was hot with bullets. His rifle was shot in two at the lower band as he was taking aim, splinters grazing his face and hands. Half the survivors had their clothing shot through, and the majority of the killed were found to have been hit two or three times.

The strength of the force was 5 officers and 184 non-commissioned officers and men, of whom 3 officers and 14 men were killed and 1 officer and 34 men were wounded.

Although the loss was great, viz. nearly one-third of the total number, it is a matter of surprise that more were not hit during the run of 130 yards, exposed as they were for about three minutes to magazine fire at a point-blank range. It can be accounted for by the fact that the Boers crouching behind the rocks were rather below than above the level of the men, and their fire being consequently directed upwards, the bullets passed high and over the heads of the charging companies. This would explain why the majority of the killed were shot through the head. Lieutenant Walker was hit in the chin, the bullet cutting his chin-strap and passing out at the back and top of his head.

The following morning, as the men were collecting and parading preparatory to marching back to the railway cutting, Sir George White rode up and addressed them. Shaking Colonel Park by the hand he said: "I congratulate and thank you for the splendid work you and your men did yesterday. It was magnificently done. I am afraid you suffered very heavily, but you must remember that such work as that cannot be done for the Empire without loss."

Whilst the three companies were performing such gallant deeds on the southern defences, the three companies under Major Curry were holding their own on the northwest defences at Observation Hill.

The Boers attacked this post heavily in the morning, and were supported by six field-guns, which were supposed to have been the Colenso

NAVAL BATTERY HILL, LADYSMITH

MONUMENT ERECTED TO DEVONS ON WAGON HILL, ON SPOT WHERE THE CHARGE TOOK PLACE, LADYSMITH

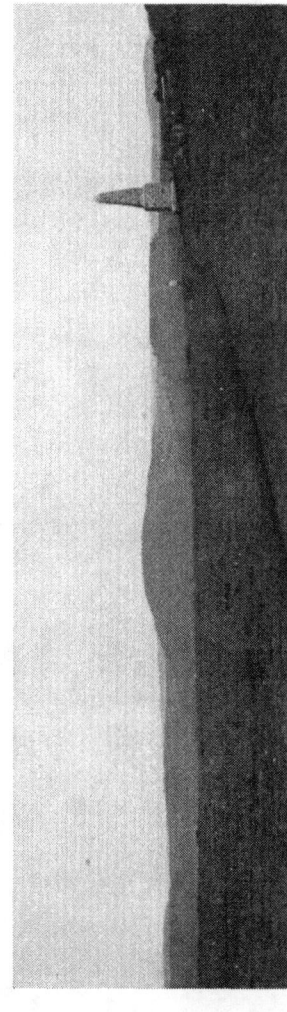

guns of General Buller's army, shrapnel being continually burst with excellent precision over the defences.

The account of the fighting which took place is told in Major Curry's own words:—

"The battle of Ladysmith commenced between 2 and 3 a.m. on Cæsar's Camp and soon we were engaged all round. The three companies which had proceeded to Observation Hill originally had just been relieved by three fresh companies. At about 4 a.m. Lieutenant Emerson reported to me that there was a party of Boers to his front, that he had fired on them, and that they had retired. I thought it was the usual picquet and that they had gone right back (it was too dark to see much); but such was not the case, for they had concealed themselves in a fold in the ground about 300 yards to our front. Their strength must have been between seventy and eighty.

"The enemy brought fire to bear on us from a 40-pounder howitzer, a field-gun, and a hotchkiss on Surprise Hill, and from one or two field-guns on the hill to our right over Hyde's Farm. They pounded away all the morning, and brought a continuous rifle fire on our position as well. At about 9.30 a.m. I heard a rattle of musketry from our centre work, and when I went up there I found that the enemy, who had concealed themselves in the fold in the ground in the early morning, had advanced right up the hill and had got within a few yards of our sangars before being seen. We killed nine and wounded twelve. They retired again to their cover, where they remained for the greater part of the day, slipping away by ones and twos back to their position. At about 4 p.m. a tremendous thunder and hail storm came on, which blotted out everything. The fire, which had ceased as the storm came on, was not renewed. Our loss was two killed by rifle fire, when the Boers made their attack. Our sangars were frequently breached by the 40-lb. shell during the day, but there was no loss from shell fire."

These three companies were relieved by the Leicesters the next evening.

Lieutenant Masterson was rewarded with the Victoria Cross, and the following is the official account of his gallant deed:—

"During the action at Wagon Hill, on the 6th January, 1900, Lieutenant Masterson

A REGIMENT OF THE LINE

commanded with the greatest gallantry and dash one of the three companies of his regiment, which charged a ridge held by the enemy, and captured the position.

"The companies were then exposed to a most heavy and galling fire from the right and left front. Lieutenant Masterson undertook to give a message to the Imperial Light Horse, who were holding a ridge some hundred yards behind, to fire to the left front and endeavour to check the enemy's fire.

"In taking this message he crossed an open space of a hundred yards, which was swept by a most heavy cross fire, and although badly wounded in both thighs managed to crawl in and deliver his message before falling exhausted into the Imperial Light Horse trench. His unselfish heroism was undoubtedly the means of saving several lives."

The gallant conduct of Colour-Sergeant Palmer was brought to notice under the following circumstances: When three companies of the Regiment were ordered to charge the ridge held by the enemy on Wagon Hill on January 6th, 1900, Colour-Sergeant Gilbert Palmer was with the leading company, and he at once dashed out to the front with most conspicuous bravery, and went straight for the point from which the heaviest fire was coming. The enemy ran before they were reached, but the three companies were exposed to a galling fire from the right, left, and front. Colour-Sergeant Palmer got behind a rock and shot several of the enemy, at the same time keeping a constant eye upon his own men, telling them when and where to fire, and when to take cover. When all the company officers were either killed or wounded, he at once recognized his position as senior non-commissioned officer, and was invaluable in getting orders passed to the other companies, and in superintending the men till dark, when the enemy retired. He then, acting under orders, personally placed the outpost line, saw to the collection of the dead and wounded, and, in fact, rendered invaluable assistance in every way.

His dash and pluck during the bayonet charge, his coolness and steady courage under a heavy cross fire, and the power of command and of quick and correct judgment displayed by him were most brilliant. Colour-Sergeant

Palmer's name was previously brought to notice for gallant conduct at the battle of Elandslaagte on October 21st, 1899, so that this made the second occasion on which he conspicuously distinguished himself.

The names of the following non-commissioned officers and men were also brought to notice for gallantry on the occasion :—

Lance-Corporal Gilbert Young.
    ,,   ,,   Frank John Rowe.
Private Henry Brimmicombe.
   ,,   R. G. Hansford.
   ,,   E. Norman.
   ,,   H. Cox.

The following message from Her Majesty the Queen was received by Sir George White for promulgation :—

"To Sir George White,
    "Ladysmith.

"Warmly congratulate you and all under your command on your brilliant success. Greatly admire conduct of Devonshire Regiment.   "V.R.I."

The following telegram was also received :—

"O/C Devon Regiment,

"Railway Cutting.

"G.O.C. directs me to convey direct to you the following message from Sir R. Buller :—

"'Congratulate all troops on gallant defence, especially Devon Regiment.'"

The losses sustained by the garrison of Ladysmith on the 6th January were :—

	Killed.	Wounded.
Officers	18	25
Men	150	224

Total killed and wounded, 417.

By the death of Captain Lafone the Regiment lost one of the kindest-hearted and best officers that ever led a company.

The Boers' losses are estimated at 64 killed and 119 wounded. This estimate may be considered low, for the *Standard and Diggers' News*, copies of which were found later on in the war, gave six full-length columns of killed and wounded amongst the various commandos.

A large donga was utilized by the Boers as a dressing station. The violent storm on the

A REGIMENT OF THE LINE

afternoon of the 6th filled all the dry dongas and turned them at once into mountain torrents. It is said that all the wounded Boers in this donga were swept out into the Klip River and drowned. The dead of the Regiment were buried with those of other regiments, in a grave under Wagon Hill. Captain Lafone and Lieutenant Field were buried in the cemetery in Ladysmith.

On the morning of January 8th all the wounded were sent by train to Intombi Camp, including Lieutenant Masterson, who was doing well.

On January 9th the Regiment was concentrated at the railway cutting, the company at the railway station having been permanently relieved from the post by a company of the Liverpool Regiment. The battalion was thus ready to be moved to any portion of the defences requiring assistance, in case of attack.

The estimation in which the battalion was held at this time by the Ladysmith garrison was well borne out by a remark made by Sir George White. "The Devons," he said, "have never failed me yet. On the 6th they held one place and took another."

A scare in the evening that the Boers were to attack again in the morning caused various preparations to be made for their advent. The garrison stood to arms at 3.15 a.m. awaiting the attack.

It is a curious fact that the Regiment was never ordered to stand to arms in the morning before three o'clock at any time previous to or after the 6th January, and the only time the Boers made a night attack they did so at 2.15 a.m. This was on January 6th, on which day the Regiment was ordered to stand to arms at 4.15 a.m.

During the night of January 9th-10th the naval guns fired in the direction of Surprise Hill, and whilst this was proceeding the mountain battery's two remaining guns also threw some star shell in the same direction. The Boers were hugely elated at the sight of the star shell. This was probably the first time they had seen them. They turned their searchlight on to the stars when they fell on the ground, and cheered lustily. They evidently considered that it was a performance got up for their special entertainment by Messrs. Brock and Co., direct from the Crystal Palace.

A REGIMENT OF THE LINE

The cause of all this shell fire was not known, but it would appear as if information had been received that the Boers had been collecting at the back of Surprise Hill the evening before, with a view to a renewed attack. Nothing, however, in the shape of an attack occurred, and at 3 a.m. firing ceased, and the sun rose in the morning in tranquillity.

On the 11th three messages were received by the garrison congratulating them on their good work of January 6th: one from the Governor of Natal, one from Valparaiso, and one from General Buller. The last named stated in his telegram that he would relieve Ladysmith as soon as possible.

It was stated that Sir George White had heliographed to Sir Redvers Buller informing him that there were over 2000 sick and wounded in Intombi Hospital Camp, that he could not hold out for much longer, and that he must not expect any assistance from him when he made his effort. Sir Redvers Buller had replied that he was sparing no effort to push forward, and that he hoped to be ready soon.

The number of patients in the Intombi Hospital Camp had increased by January 10th to—

Over 400 cases of dysentery;
,, 600 cases of enteric fever;
,, 200 cases not yet diagnosed, but probably enteric fever;
,, 800 cases wounded and various.

The daily rations of the garrison now consisted of ½ lb. of tinned meat and 1 lb. of bread per man.

Had it not been for the Indian Contingent there would have been no flour at all in Ladysmith. All the flour, all the rum, in fact almost everything that the garrison lived upon with the exception of meat, was brought from India with the Indian Contingent, which carried with it six months' supply of every description.

From January 12th, another duty assigned to the Regiment was the sending of two companies every morning at two o'clock to the examining guard on the Newcastle road, which was situated just under the 4·7 naval gun "Lady Anne." They had orders to stop there till

A PEACEFUL SUNDAY
KLIP RIVER AND CAMP OF THE IMPERIAL LIGHT HORSE, LADYSMITH

A REGIMENT OF THE LINE

4.30 a.m. to check any rush of Boers into Ladysmith down the Newcastle road. Later on, the ground in front of this post was covered with barbed wire entanglement, but up to this time there was nothing at this point to prevent the Boers galloping right into the town.

As these two companies went to their places on the 12th, the Boer searchlight on Bulwana was flashing everywhere, and the mountain guns throwing star shell. It looked as if both sides expected an attack. The officer commanding the two companies had orders to operate on the flank of any attack made on the northern defences.

On the following morning the garrison was told that General Buller was moving round by Springfield; in the evening it was given out that he was moving west of Chieveley and Colenso, and was twelve miles from Ladysmith; and on the 14th the news came in that he was at Potgieter's Drift, and that General Warren was across the Tugela River; and in confirmation of this last information heavy gun fire was heard on the 17th in the direction of Potgieters, and the relieving army's balloon was seen on the following day in the same direction.

As an attack was expected on the night of the 19th on Observation Hill, three companies of the Regiment under Major Curry proceeded there in the evening and bivouacked, the remainder of the Regiment being under orders to hold themselves in readiness to proceed there at a moment's notice. The night, however, passed quietly, and the companies returned to their camp before dawn.

On January 20th better news was received from Sir Redvers Buller; his advance had been very satisfactory. Reports stated that he had reached Acton Holmes, and that four brigades had crossed the Tugela. His shells were seen falling thickly on Thabba Nyama mountain.

The tea and sugar rations were, however, cut down to half. The health of the men began now to generally improve, probably owing to better drinking water which was obtainable from the condenser, recently arranged for, at the railway station.

Very heavy gun fire, night and day, was continually heard from the direction of Spion

Kop and Acton Holmes, and on the 23rd a demonstration was made from Ladysmith, the mounted troops going out under cover of the fire of all the guns. The Ladysmith guns on all the fronts opened, but were answered only by the Boer guns on Gun Hill and Bulwana. There was but little musketry fire from Pepworth direction, and Surprise Hill seemed deserted.

Still no relief appeared, and the rations were :—

> 12 oz. of beef.
> 1 lb. of bread.
> Half ration of sugar.
> Half ration of tea.

An order published on the 23rd gave hope :—

"Sir George White has received further satisfactory news as to Sir R. Buller's advance. The relief of Ladysmith may be said to be within measurable distance."

Very heavy gun fire was heard from 3 a.m. on the 24th till 2 p.m., and in the evening further encouragement was circulated :—

"Reassuring news has been received from Sir R. Buller."

No news from the relieving army was received on the 25th. Heavy firing continued, and in the evening the Boers were seen trekking from the direction of Spion Kop, all the laagers on the rear slopes of the mountain clearing off and making for Vanreenen's Pass and Newcastle. In fact, the whole country round Spion Kop seemed about to be hurriedly abandoned by the Boers. Great excitement prevailed in Ladysmith.

An investigation of the slopes of Spion Kop through the glasses at daybreak on the following morning proved, however, disappointing, for the laagers which had cleared off the night before were back again in their places. Moreover, the Boers round Ladysmith were very truculent on the morning of the 26th, which necessitated the garrison standing to arms till 6 a.m.

Prices at the weekly auction had gone up considerably.

Two vegetable marrows were sold for 5s. 6d.

Pumpkins fetched 2s. 6d. each.

A small plate of potatoes reached 11s.

Whilst four sticks (4 oz.) of black tobacco, "Fair-maid" brand, changed hands at £5 10s.

From now till the end of the siege two companies of the Regiment were moved to a healthier spot, known as the "Convalescent Camp." It was situated at the eastern end of Convent Hill. This post was relieved weekly, and as the men were concealed and in a healthier position the change was much appreciated.

On the morning of January 27th a native runner brought in news. His account was :—

"Boers lost heavily from artillery fire on Wednesday, and say that the British artillery is too much for them. I saw six field cornets dead on one wagon. Some English were taken prisoners, and they were from the left flank attack. The English attacked Spion Kop and surrounded the base of the hill, and the Boers lost heavily from the English shrapnel fire. When the English got to the top of the hill the Boers ran down the other side. The Boers are much disheartened by their losses."

Judging from the above, the native must

have then run away and not have waited to see the finish, for in the evening the following news came in :—

"Buller attacked Spion Kop, seized and occupied it, but was driven off again the next night. Our loss is estimated at 200 killed and 300 wounded."

With the knowledge that history has given the world about the battle of Spion Kop, further comment is needless. The news above is given as it was received by the garrison of Ladysmith, who of course knew nothing but what was sent in in scraps by Sir Redvers Buller, and what came in to the Intelligence Department by native runners.

On the 30th the daily ration was further cut down to ½ lb. of meat, 2 biscuits, ⅙ oz. of tea, and ½ oz. of sugar per man. Horses, except those belonging to the artillery, went rationless.

On January 31st horse-flesh was issued for the first time as a ration.

One dozen whisky was raffled in the town, and fetched £144—£1 10s. per wineglass!

A REGIMENT OF THE LINE 87

The only news received from the outside world on February 2nd was that—

"Sir R. Buller has retired behind the Tugela to rearrange, and Sir John Lubbock has been made a peer."

The question asked is, Who is Lubbock, and is he connected in any way with the evacuation of Spion Kop?

Some say that the news is the wrong way about, and that Lubbock has retired and Sir R. Buller been made a peer. Confirmation of the news was anxiously awaited.

Whichever way it was, in the face of the evacuation of Spion Kop it was poor news to feed a half-starved and anxious garrison on. However, in the meantime the big gun on Bulwana had fired his great shells into the Railway Cutting Camp and killed the doctor's horse.

About this time a decoction called "chevril" was issued to the men. It was supplied by the 18th Hussars' horses, whose bodies were boiled down for the purpose. It was nourishing and the men liked it, which was a good thing. There was nothing else by which to recommend it. The men were also allowed to go down to the chevril factory, which was close to the station, and buy the flesh of the horse after it had passed through the boiling process. This did not appear appetizing, but again the men liked it, and when cooked up with wild spinach which grew about the lines it was considered very tasty.

Two items of news were received on February 4th, one being that General Buller had again crossed the Tugela in three places and was to be expected shortly, and the other that the garrison of Ladysmith was to be attacked again next morning by 10,000 Boers. Arrangements were made to meet the latter, the arrival of the former being considered hypothetical. The garrison stood to arms at three o'clock the following morning and anxiously awaited the dawn, but everything went off quietly, and at 5.30 a.m. General Buller's guns commenced in three different directions. The sound of the heavy gun fire increased in intensity, till at 2.30 p.m. the noise could be compared to a heavy storm with incessant thunder.

The Regiment was now told off as part of

a flying column. This was hopeful, as it was supposed that arrangements were being made to co-operate with the relieving army.

At 5.15 a.m. on the 5th Buller's guns began firing again and continued the whole day.

For the next few days there was no news from the outside world. Buller's guns were heard incessantly, and one Boer big gun was seen firing on Dornkloof, south of Manger's Hill. A few of Buller's lyddite shells were bursting near him, and one shell was seen to strike his magazine and explode it.

On the seventh night 100 men of the Regiment were again engaged in shifting the 4·7 gun "Lady Anne."

On the 9th nothing was heard of Buller's guns—perfect silence!

This gave rise to all sorts of reports, one actually given out being that Buller had taken his position and could come in at any time he liked, but he had been stopped by a telegram from the Cape in order to allow of Lord Roberts pushing up through the Free State; and then both Buller and Roberts would relieve Ladysmith and take Bloemfontein respectively on the same day. And this on the very day on which Buller was retiring south of Tugela again from Vaal Krantz.

It was now considered advisable to strengthen the defences held by the Regiment by an additional work, and the men were kept hard at it from 7.15 p.m. till 10 p.m. A dish of chevril was served out to each man of the working party before turning in.

On February 13th information was received that Buller had taken two positions on the north side of the Tugela with small loss—one Krantz Kloof, and the other Vaal Krantz Spruit. This information seemed somewhat belated. A message was also received from Lord Roberts in which he stated that he had entered the Free State with a very large force, chiefly of artillery and cavalry, and hoped that the pressure on Ladysmith would shortly be reduced. Heavy gun fire commenced in the Colenso direction on the night of February 14th, and continued with slight interruption till the 18th; and on the 15th the Boer pom-pom was heard in action, which went to show that the opposing forces were not very far from each other.

A REGIMENT OF THE LINE

At the last public auction ever held in the town, i.e. on the 14th evening, the prices were :—

> Eggs, 48s. per dozen.
> Vegetable marrows, 28s. each.
> Mealies, 3s. 8d. each.
> Pot of jam, 32s. 6d.
> Crosse & Blackwell's piccalilli, 19s. 6d.
> Tin of ox tongue, 20s. 6d.
> 2 oz. stick of cake tobacco, 22s.
> Fifty cigars, 10 guineas.

As much as 25s. per stick was paid about this time for two ounces of cake tobacco. No Kaffir leaf tobacco was to be bought in the town, although as much as £5 per leaf was offered.

On the 15th the Railway Cutting Camp again received the attention of the Long Tom gunners on Bulwana, who pitched some shells into the lines, but without doing damage.

The news of the relief of Kimberley was received by the garrison on February 17th, and it was reported that General French had captured five laagers.

On Sunday, the 18th, the battalion and 13th

Battery, the remains of the Gloucester Regiment, and the Mountain Battery assembled as usual under "Liverpool Castle" for Divine service. The Reverend J. Tuckey officiated. The usual "extermination" service and prayers for the "Right" were said, the hymns chosen being—

> There is a blessed home
> Beyond this land of woe;

and

> There is a green hill far away,

sung sadly to the accompaniment of Buller's guns.

He appears to be nearer, and his shells have been bursting on a hill and ridge in the distance, Colenso way.

The following statistics are of interest :—

Early in November the garrison of Ladysmith numbered about 13,500 men. During the siege there were over 10,500 admissions to hospital.

Thirty-eight men had been killed by shell fire, and 430 men had died of disease. Four shells only had accounted for nearly all the thirty-eight.

A REGIMENT OF THE LINE

On February 19th news was sent in that General Buller had captured Cingolo Mountain and Monte Christo, and that excellent progress was being made by him. The Boers were seen trekking north all day; and in the evening Buller's heliographs were seen flashing from Monte Christo, and two guns on the same hill firing at the Boers. With the exception of Buller's heliograph and balloon this was the first occasion that the relieving army was seen from Ladysmith.

On February 22nd, with the intention of finding out whether there had been any reduction in the investing force, the Regiment with some mounted infantry were ordered to reconnoitre in the direction of Flag Hill. A start was made at 3.30 a.m. Some sixty Boers were encountered, and the Regiment was ordered back to camp at 6.15 a.m., fired at by the sixty Boers.

Buller's guns were heard firing incessantly all day and every day. His shells were now seen bursting on a southern spur of Bulwana and near Intombi Camp.

During the siege the Boers conceived the idea of flooding the Ladysmith plain and the town by damming the Klip River below Intombi Camp. This dam was commenced towards the end of the siege, but was not completed when Ladysmith was relieved. It was a good target for the naval 12-pounder guns on Cæsar's Camp, which frequently fired at it. These in their turn received on such occasions a good deal of attention from the Boer big gun on Bulwana.

On the night of the 24th the 4·7 gun "Lady Anne" was again moved; this was for the fourth and the last time. On the same night very heavy rifle and Maxim gun fire was heard on the hills south of Cæsar's Camp. This continued for about one hour, when the firing was taken up by the Boer outposts all round Ladysmith, a few bullets reaching the Convalescent Camp on Convent Hill.

February 27th being Majuba Day, the garrison, expecting a demonstration from the Boers, stood to arms at 4.15 a.m., but, much to the astonishment of everybody, not a shot was fired. General Buller sent the garrison in the following message :—

"Colenso rail bridge, which was totally destroyed, is under repair ; road bridge partially destroyed ; am doing very well, but the country is difficult and my progress is slow ; hope to be with you soon."

Official news was also received that Lord Roberts had surrounded Cronje, who had surrendered with 4000 Boers, the English losses being given as 1700 killed and wounded.

On the 28th rations were further cut down to one biscuit and three ounces of mealies, with one pound of horse as before per man. This was perhaps the most distressing circumstance connected with the siege, and it had a most depressing effect. It was not so much the reduction of the ration that was of consequence, as the reason for the reduction. This could not be guessed at, and it gave rise to conjectures, the chief being that Buller had again failed, and could not get through. His shells had been seen bursting on the hills, and that had encouraged the garrison ; but the garrison had been encouraged before by the sight of Buller's shells bursting on Thabba Nyama. Three days previously, owing to the good news received from Buller, the garrison had been put on full rations, but now, after further good news, the order was promulgated :—

"Highly satisfactory reports have been sent from General Buller as to his advance, but the country is difficult and progress slow, therefore I am obliged to reduce the ration, etc. etc."

This sudden cancelling of the increase of the ration, and its still further reduction in the face of the news received and in the sight of Buller's shells, was disappointing. Having ascertained that the garrison could exist till April 15th and not longer, and that then there would not be a horse, ox, or mule left, Sir George White, much against his will, but to make things certain in case General Buller was again checked, gave the orders for the reduction on the day before the relief.

During the day the big gun on Bulwana made an attempt to reach Observation Hill Post, which were the furthest works from him in that direction. His attempt succeeded, and he put many shells into the works. His record for the siege was an attempt to reach

A REGIMENT OF THE LINE

Wagon Hill. He failed in this, but his range, as measured on the map, was 11,560 yards, or 6 miles and 1000 yards.

February 28th, the last day of the siege, was very hot and oppressive; everybody seemed depressed, trying to guess at some reason for the ration reduction. At about 2 p.m., however, Major Riddel, brigade-major to Colonel Knox, came up to the officers' mess smiling all over, and said that excellent news, the very best, had come in, but that "*it is confidential, and I am not allowed to say what it is.*" He called for volunteers who were willing and able to march seven miles and fight at the end of it. The whole Regiment, officers and men, volunteered, but after a medical examination had been made of the battalion, only one hundred men were found to come up to requirements.

At about 3.30 p.m. the news was distributed that General Buller had gained a complete victory over the Boers, who were in full retreat. Hundreds of wagons were seen going off north towards Modder Station and Vanreenens, and at 4 p.m. a derrick was seen hoisted over the big gun on

Bulwana, and the naval guns opened fire on him. The Boers dismounted him under a heavy fire from one 4·7 and two naval 12-pounders, and got him away.

At 6.20 p.m. a welcome sight greeted the eyes of the weary garrison, for suddenly out of the bush appeared two squadrons of mounted men, riding leisurely in across the plain from the direction of Intombi, and the truth dawned on the garrison that Ladysmith was at last and in reality relieved.

The siege had lasted four calendar months to the day.

Frantic cheering greeted them as they crossed the ford and reached the town.

On the following day a column, consisting of the Devons, Gordon Highlanders, three batteries of artillery, all the cavalry who had horses, and the two mounted colonial corps, the whole under the command of Colonel W. G. Knox, sallied forth at 10 a.m. towards Modder Station to pursue and to stop the Boers getting their big guns away by train. On arriving abreast of Pepworth Hill, which the Boer rear-guard had occupied, the advanced troops, consisting of Devons and the batteries,

A REGIMENT OF THE LINE

came under rather a sharp fire. All further progress was stopped, and the column returned to camp. The Devons had two men wounded. Camp was reached at 4.30 p.m. The battalion was met on the way home by Major Davies, Captains Bols and Vigors, Lieutenants Lafone and Munro, all of the 2nd Battalion. These had ridden in from their camp, and brought with them tobacco, whisky, rum, and milk. The companies of the 2nd Battalion sent in to their corresponding companies tea, sugar, tobacco, matches, etc. These were all most eagerly accepted.

Sir Redvers Buller and his staff rode into Ladysmith in the afternoon.

Explosions at Modder Station and on the railway could be heard, signifying that the Boers were making good their retreat by blowing up the bridges.

On March 3rd General Buller made his public entry into Ladysmith at the head of his army. The march of Buller's army through Ladysmith was a pageant which those who took part in the siege will never forget.

The garrison of Ladysmith lined the streets.

Sir George White with his staff took his stand mounted, under the damaged clock tower of the Town Hall—the Gordons on the one hand, the Devons on the other—the Gordon pipers facing him on the opposite side of the road.

It was a great sight, and those who had been through the siege and had heard the words of their leader at the end, "Thank God we have kept the flag flying," knew it for a great sight.

General Buller rode at the head of his army, and received an immense ovation, as did all his regiments and artillery as they passed through the lines of the weedy, sickly-looking garrison. These with their thin, pale faces cheered to the full bent of their power, but after standing in the sun for some time they became exhausted, and Sir Redvers sent back word for them to sit down, which they gladly did, whilst the relievers, as they passed along, chucked them bits of tobacco, ready cut up, from their small store, small because they themselves were also hard put for luxuries.

The tramp! tramp! of these men, who to

A REGIMENT OF THE LINE

the weakly garrison appeared as veritable giants, will never be forgotten, as they hurried past to the strains of the Gordons' pipes, cheering with the utmost enthusiasm the figure of Sir George White as they passed him. They were almost to a man reservists, well covered, hard, and well set up. They were filthy, their clothes were mended and patched, and most of them had scrubby beards. Tied on to their belts in almost all cases was a Boer blanket, telling that they had been busy in some Boer laager; on the top of this a small bundle of sticks for each man to cook his own tea, and by his side, attached to his belt, hung his black tin pot. But how well they looked—the picture of vigour, health, and strength, as they "tramp, tramp"—"tramp, tramp" through the town.

A corps that came in for a good deal of notice was the Bearer Company. They were at first taken for Boer prisoners, but when it became known who they were they were much cheered. Clad in worn-out "slops" they slouched along, in each man's hand a pot of sorts, enamel or china, and a bundle of something over each man's shoulder.

The meeting of the two battalions was not quite so emotional as has been depicted by some authors. The 2nd Battalion, the relievers, came through late at the rear of Buller's army, and by that time the 1st Battalion, the relieved, had been in the sun, standing or sitting down on the curbstone, for some hours, and a great many men had fallen out exhausted. Still the meeting was very hearty, officers recognizing men and men old comrades. There was little time to enact the scene so graphically described by one author "which would make old men weep." Buller's army was straggled out a good deal and the rear had to catch up, so if a pal was seen he was gone next moment to give way to another pal. Most of the reservists had been through the ranks of the 1st Battalion, and with it through the Tirah Campaign; almost all were hurriedly recognized, and a hearty and hasty shake of the hand was all the greeting exchanged. Old jokes came to the fore, and were bandied from one to the other as the 2nd Battalion hurried along. There was no time for more—one battalion was in a hurry and the other exhausted.

DEVON OFFICERS REMAINING FIT FOR DUTY AT THE END OF THE SIEGE
(Rajab—Regimental Barber)

It was well on in the day before the 1st Battalion got back to its camp at the Railway Cutting.

On Sunday, March 4th, a Thanksgiving Service was held on the flat ground between the Convent Hill and the Naval Brigade Hill, which was attended by Generals Buller and White, and on its conclusion the battalion moved into tents outside the works and in front of Gloucester Post.

It was a strange experience moving out into the open, away from the protection of the works. The nerves of most had had a severe strain from want of food and continual anxiety.

It was the anxiety which killed. There is nothing more conducive to the deterioration of men's minds than false alarms on an empty stomach.

CHAPTER III

EVENTS FOLLOWING THE SIEGE OF LADYSMITH, AND THE ADVANCE NORTH UNDER SIR REDVERS BULLER

1900

THE first few days following the relief were employed in the sorting and reading of four months' mails and the opening up of presents. Many complimentary telegrams were received by the battalion from England.

Major Davies, Captain Bartlett, and Lieutenant Willis, all of whom had been doing duty with the 2nd Battalion during the relief operations, joined the battalion on the 7th with some eighty-six men who had been sent from Jullunder.

The two battalions were together for a few days only, as the 2nd Battalion after a short rest proceeded with Sir Redvers Buller's force towards Modder Spruit.

BRIGADIER-GENERAL WALTER KITCHENER

On March 10th the Ladysmith garrison was reorganized, the battalion being placed in the 7th Brigade with the Gordon Highlanders, the Manchester Regiment, and the 2nd Battalion Rifle Brigade. This brigade was commanded by Colonel W. G. Knox, C.B.

Colonel Park, unfortunately struck down with enteric fever on the last day of the siege, was shortly afterwards invalided to England. In his absence Major Davies took over command of the battalion, and Major Curry having been appointed Commandant of Ladysmith, Captain Jacson took over the duties of Second-in-Command. On March 14th the 7th Brigade marched to Arcadia, seven miles out of Ladysmith on the Vanreenen's Pass road, camping on a kopje overlooking Dewdrop Spruit. The men were then occupied in route marching and generally getting fit.

Brigadier-General Walter Kitchener arrived in camp on the 26th March and took over the command of the 7th Brigade from Colonel Knox, and on April 2nd the battalion, accompanied by General W. Kitchener, marched to Brakfontein, seventeen miles distant under Spion Kop, stopped there in camp on the 3rd, when parties of men went off to view the Boer positions on Spion Kop and Vaal-Krantz, and returned to Arcadia on the 4th.

Innumerable presents were continually arriving from England for the battalion, and the thanks of all are due especially to Mr. Young of Torquay for the indefatigable manner in which he worked, and for the numerous bundles and boxes of presents which he was instrumental in collecting and dispatching both at this time and also afterwards. All these presents were highly appreciated.

A draft of 180 men, consisting of reservists, section "D" Militia Reservists, and recruits joined the battalion on the 7th; amongst these were 120 married men.

At 11.30 a.m. on April 11th orders were received to move at once into Ladysmith, which was to be reached at 2 p.m. The reason for the sudden move was not explained. There was no transport. Out of six wagons, the complement for a battalion on light field service scale, there were only two in camp at the time. At Arcadia the battalion, in common with the rest of the brigade, was allowed tents, and told that it could have any-

A REGIMENT OF THE LINE

thing it liked to take with it. There was consequently a good deal more than six carts could carry.

Towards evening, after the tents had been struck, packed, and sent on ahead, and the battalion was waiting in the open for more wagons, a most violent thunderstorm came on, lasting about two hours. Ten men of one company which was holding a work on Rifleman's Ridge, between Arcadia and Ladysmith, were struck by lightning, none, however, being killed. The battalion eventually reached camp at Star Hill, just above the iron bridge outside Ladysmith, at 3 a.m. wet to the skin. It was found that the tents had arrived. These were pitched and the men turned in. The greater part of the brigade did not reach Star Hill till the following day.

On the 13th the Gordons and Devons moved camp to Hyde's Farm under Surprise Hill, the Devons proceeding next day to a camp under Thornhill's Kopje, throwing out picquets on that hill and also on another kopje further out towards Nicholson's Nek known as Devon Kopje.

From this time till May 15th the battalion

remained quietly encamped under Thornhill's Kopje. Route marching and field days occupied the men most mornings, hockey and football most afternoons. The men suffered a good deal at first from jaundice, which was chiefly the result of over-eating after their long abstinence, but they got fit and recovered their strength gradually; it was, however, fully six weeks to two months before they were really ready to take the field.

In the meantime General Buller had turned the Biggarsberg, and the Boers had fallen back on Laing's Nek.

The 7th Brigade now formed part of the 4th Division under the command of Major-General Neville Lyttleton, and on May 16th the Regiment was ordered to proceed north to Modder's Spruit. Here it remained till the 20th, on which day it continued its march to Elandslaagte, and encamped near the railway station. On the 23rd, having handed in all tents and excess baggage, the Regiment marched to Sunday's River, where it joined up with the divisional head-quarters, and on the following day formed the rear-guard on the march to Black Craig Farm. Here

RAILWAY BRIDGE DESTROYED BY BOERS, INGAGANE

A REGIMENT OF THE LINE

the division encamped in the heart of the Biggarsberg.

Halting at Kalabis on the 25th, the division reached Ingagane on the 26th.

The brigade was now split up and placed on the line of communications, and it was thought probable that the Regiment would see no more fighting and that the war would soon be brought to a conclusion. Of the four regiments in the brigade, the Manchester Regiment had been left behind to garrison Jonono's Kop and the railway line near Elandslaagte, the Devons were left to garrison Ingagane on the railway, and the Rifle Brigade was at Newcastle and between that place and Ingogo at the foot of the Laing's Nek pass. The Gordon Highlanders were at Ingogo and guarded the railway line still further north.

The Regiment itself was also split up. A detachment of one company under Captain Travers (increased afterwards to two companies) proceeded to occupy Dannhauser, and two companies under Captain Bartlett were ordered to Rooi Pint on the high ground between Ingagane and Newcastle. A battery of artillery was also stationed at this place.

The remaining companies of the Regiment, including a 9th or K company which had been created shortly after the siege, were posted on the low hill overlooking Ingagane railway station.

On June 4th the 1st Cavalry Brigade arrived to form part of the garrison of Ingagane. This brigade was commanded by Brigadier-General Burn Murdoch, who was in charge of the line of communication Newcastle-Dannhauser.

At Ingagane Hill the Regiment found itself again employed in building stone walls. Entrenchments against attack were considered necessary, for it was thought probable that the Boers would attempt to break through from the north-east of the Free State on the west and cross into Utrecht and Vryheid districts. The real danger, however, lay on the east, for the Vryheid district long remained a Boer stronghold, and parties of Boers frequently raided to the Blood River in the immediate neighbourhood of Dannhauser.

It was owing to this that on June 15th a second company was sent to reinforce Captain Travers at Dannhauser. The hill selected by

MAKING BARBED-WIRE ENTANGLEMENT, INGAGANE

A REGIMENT OF THE LINE

Captain Travers for defence overlooked Dannhauser railway station, and commanded a large extent of ground to the east of the post. This hill was very strongly fortified, and the works on it, designed and built by Captain Travers and his men, were perhaps the best works for protection against musketry fire constructed by the Regiment during the war.

News was received daily that thousands of Boers with dozens of guns were on the eastern flank, with every intention of raiding, cutting the line, and attacking Dannhauser. Dundee also, according to the newspapers and the evidence of native scouts, was in deadly peril from attack by Chris. Botha. It was, perhaps, on account of these rumours that a column was formed to reconnoitre Utrecht. In conjunction with another column which moved out from Ingogo, three companies of the Regiment, with the Royal Dragoons and the 5th Dragoon Guards and two field guns, moved out on the afternoon of July 1st from Ingagane and camped at Tundega Farm. On the following morning Tundega Hill was occupied by the infantry whilst the cavalry reconnoitred over the Buffalo River to Utrecht, which was distant twenty miles. This place was found occupied by about four hundred Boers, and after some skirmishing and a good deal of firing the cavalry returned with a loss of one Royal Dragoon taken prisoner. Next morning the force returned to Ingagane. The operations were supposed to have been very successful.

By the end of July the Regiment had quite recovered tone and vigour, and was well and fit for any work, and on August 2nd, 1900, orders were received to pack up and proceed by rail the following day to Zandspruit. On the afternoon of the 3rd the Regiment entrained in coal trucks for the north. Majuba and Laing's Nek were passed next morning at dawn, and at 7.30 a.m. Zandspruit was reached.

The strength of the battalion was now 938 of all ranks. All tents and excess baggage had been returned to store, and on the 6th the Regiment marched to Meerzicht, where the remainder of General Lyttleton's 4th Division was found in bivouac. The 4th Division was now complete and ready to march north with Sir Redvers Buller.

General Buller's force moved out from Meerzicht on August 7th. For some days previously the Boers had been occupying in force some high ground known as Rooi Kopjes, a few miles north of Meerzicht, and the Gordon Highlanders had already twice been slightly engaged with them. The 7th Brigade advanced out of their camp in attack formation, the Gordons leading the advance, the Devons in support. Their objective was the Rooi Kopjes. These were found unoccupied, and, having gained the summit, the 7th Brigade were ordered to make a sweep round to the right.

The new objective was the high ground above Amersfoort. General Buller's line now occupied some five miles of front. A very high wind was blowing, and it was not for some time that the Head-quarter Staff, who at the time were with the 7th Brigade, knew that the artillery of the 8th Brigade, which had marched direct on Amersfoort, were in action, firing at some Boer guns mounted on the Amersfoort Hills. The Boers were strongly entrenched on these hills to the number of about 3000 to 4000 with fourteen guns under

Chris. Botha and D. Joubert. The 7th Brigade advanced across a large undulating plain, the Devons leading. The Gordons had been sent round to the left to support Dundonald's Mounted Brigade, who had been checked by some fifty Boers. About 6000 yards from the position Boer shells began to fall among the companies of the leading battalion. One half battalion under Major Davies thereupon opened out and advanced, while the other half battalion was sent to the left under Captain Jacson, with orders to proceed as rapidly as possible to the assistance of the Gordon Highlanders, who, it was reported, were being heavily threatened by the Boers on the extreme left. With the exception of some shell fire the main advance was continued unopposed. The left half battalion of the Regiment had to make a very long detour, and on its arrival to the assistance of the Gordons it was found that the Boer force, which was threatening the left flank, was simply Dundonald's mounted troops drawing up stationary behind some rising ground.

After a stiff climb the summit of the Amersfoort Hills was reached just before dark.

It was found that the Boers had evacuated their position, on their left flank and rear being threatened by the 8th Brigade. The leading battalion of this brigade, the 60th Rifles, came under some heavy musketry fire from the houses in the town, and after several casualties, which included four officers, Major Campbell, commanding the 60th, threatened to burn the town if the firing was not discontinued. The firing then ceased, and the Boers retired to the hills north of the town.

The Boers had set fire to the long dry grass in every direction, and it was chiefly by the light of these fires that regiments, companies, and parties of mounted men found their way off the hill on a pitch-dark night.

No orders had been circulated as to where the force was to halt and bivouac for the night, and from every direction various bodies of men groped their way in the dark towards the town, in the hopes that when once there some orders might be obtained. It was late when the half battalion under Captain Jacson found its bivouac and joined hands again with that of Major Davies just outside the town.

One company came in later, having unfortunately lost its way in the dark.

Some of the leading wagons of the transport, which had been sent along the direct road from Meerzicht to Amersfoort, broke down in a bad drift, thus blocking the remainder. No wagons arrived in Amersfoort that night, and the men after their long tramp, a continuous march without a halt from 7.30 a.m. till about 8.30 at night, were without greatcoats or blankets. The night was bitterly cold, with a hard frost. Gangs of men went down to the town and brought back wood. Soon fires began to light up in the Devons' and Gordons' bivouacs, which were adjoining, and for the remainder of the night groups of men sat round them trying to keep warm. The four companies of the Regiment on outpost duty suffered very severely, as they were without fires, none being allowed in the outpost line.

The force halted at Amersfoort on the following day, owing firstly to the fog which enveloped everything, and secondly to allow of the baggage train coming up. This began to arrive at 10 a.m., having been detained at the drift the whole night.

THE BAGGAGE OF GENERAL BULLER'S ARMY CROSSING BEGINDERLYN BRIDGE

During the fog a few Boers came down from the high ground above the river and fired into the horses watering, at very close range. They failed, however, to do any damage.

On August 9th the army continued its advance. On leaving Amersfoort, a bad drift with a steep climb of half a mile on the further side was met with, and the baggage was formed into two columns. This was assisted up the hill by two companies of the Regiment, Sir Redvers Buller personally superintending. Klippaal Drift was reached late in the afternoon after a difficult march of ten miles.

General Buller's army was now on the high veldt in winter time. The cold was intense, especially at night, when there were several degrees of frost. Owing to the intense cold, two men of the Rifle Brigade died from exposure during the night.

On the following day the force continued its march to Beginderlyn Bridge. This was found intact, and there was no opposition, and the march was resumed on the 11th as far as Kleinfontein. On August 12th Ermelo was occupied, and a few of the leading Boers belonging to the place surrendered.

So far, and until Twyfelaar was reached, Buller's army received little or no opposition from the Boers. Chris. Botha, who had occupied Amersfoort, had retired east after evacuating that place, and was marching parallel to the British force and at a distance of about ten miles on its right flank. They were evidently watching Buller, probably thinking that he would turn east towards Piet Retief, where almost all their stock, sheep, and cattle had been driven, the mountainous and difficult country there being suitable for its concealment and protection.

The main body of the Boers was concentrated between Belfast and Machadodorp, north-east of Twyfelaar, in a country eminently suited for what was considered their final effort. The valley of the Komati River was exceedingly difficult country for the British army to operate over. The Boers to the end of the war were very fond of this country, and it was there, or in the vicinity towards Lake Chrissie, that several engagements took place later on, during the guerilla

A REGIMENT OF THE LINE

stage of the war, not always in favour of the British.

The town of Ermelo, which the Regiment was destined to see again on several future occasions, was left on August 13th, on the evening of which day the force reached Klipfontein. The Regiment, being rear-guard, did not reach its bivouac till after dark. Witbank was reached the following day, and communication was opened up with General French's column, fifteen miles to the north-west. Carolina could be seen eight miles away to the north-east.

The force marched next day to Twyfelaar, and here a halt was made till August 21st, in order to allow of Lord Roberts's army, which was advancing east from Pretoria along the Lorenzo Marques railway, joining hands with General Buller's army.

The rear-guard of the force was attacked by the Boers on August 21st on its march from Twyfelaar to Van Wycks Vlei. The Gordon Highlanders lost nine killed and eight wounded, and the Liverpool Mounted Infantry eight killed.

On the following morning a force consisting

of Devons, Manchesters, Gordons, South African Light Horse, one field battery, and the howitzers, advanced from Van Wycks Vlei under General W. Kitchener, for the purpose of reconnoitring and driving some Boers off the hills east of General Buller's camp, so that the road for the next day's march might be cleared of the enemy. A large number of Boers was seen in the direction of Carolina, and it was supposed that Chris. Botha's force was opposed to the column. The Manchester Regiment led the advance, supported by the Devon Regiment. The former, on crossing a nek to a low underlying hill, came under a heavy rifle fire from the Boers below and across the valley, and lost two killed and nine wounded. The force returned to camp at 6 p.m.

On the following day Buller's army advanced to Geluk, some five or six miles, the battalion with the Gordons and mounted troops of Dundonald's Brigade, acting as rear-guard. A very difficult spruit, with steep sides, was crossed, and the high hills on the further side occupied. These had been held by the Boers in strength, but they had retired on Buller's approach. As soon as the infantry of the rear-guard had arrived in camp, the mounted troops of the rear-guard were attacked rather sharply, but they managed to hold their own and to beat off the Boers. Two companies of the Liverpool Regiment, who formed part of the advance guard, fell into an ambush and lost considerably, leaving, it was reported, some eighty men either killed, wounded, or prisoners in the hands of the Boers. Shortly after arrival in camp, five companies of the Regiment were sent out on outpost duty, taking up a short line and entrenching—two companies were entrenched in front and furnished sentries, with three companies entrenched in rear in support.

On August 24th and 25th the force stood fast, exchanging occasional big gun and musketry fire with the Boers. Information was received that Lord Roberts had entered Belfast on the 24th, thus practically joining hands with Sir Redvers Buller.

The position taken up by the Boers already referred to, an immensely powerful one, straddled the Pretoria-Lorenzo railway east of Belfast and west of Machadodorp. Botha had taken up a front of some fifty miles in length, and his force numbered about 5000 men. His right rested on the broken mountainous country of Elandskloof to the north, and his left on the mountains overlooking the Komati to the south. His centre was at Bergendal Farm and the rugged and precipitous hills in the rear of the farm, through which wound the railway and road, his line of retreat, quite concealed from the fire and view of the British force. On the extreme left a big gun with two or three smaller pieces were mounted, but these were useless to give much support to the centre, as they were too distant. The line of retreat to Komati Poort, which, from the nature of the country, could not be threatened except by an extended movement round the north or south, lay along the Belfast-Machadodorp road and the railway line.

Briefly, the course of the two days' battle may be described as follows :—

While Pole Carew threatened the centre at Belfast and the position north of the railway, French was sent with his cavalry division still further north to threaten the Boer line of retreat towards Pilgrim's Rest, and their right flank. Buller attacked the Boers' left with the intention of driving it in and getting behind their centre on their line of retreat. He on the first day, however, could make no impression on them, and the two forces held on to the position they were in for the night. On the morning of the second day Buller, leaving a brigade of infantry and Dundonald's mounted brigade to watch the Boers' left, moved across their front under cover of the undulating slopes of ground, and made an attack at Bergendal Farm and Kopje. After a sharp fight this was carried, and the Boers retired all along their line in the direction of Machadodorp.

It is necessary to state in detail the part played by the Regiment.

On the morning of Sunday, August 26th, Buller's force was put in motion. The Regiment was advance guard to the division. When about half a mile from the camp, the four advanced and extended companies under Captain Jacson came under fire from some high ground on their right flank, losing two men. Major Davies, proceeding along this ridge of high ground with the remainder of the Regiment, forced the Boers posted there off the hills. The advance guard companies then continued their march with orders to make Bergendal Farm their point, but not to go beyond it.

When these companies had proceeded some four or five miles, it was found that General Buller's main body had changed direction to the right and had gone east. On retracing their steps, the companies with great difficulty ascertained the whereabouts of Buller's force. Sir Redvers was now attacking the Boer left within a mile or two of his former camping ground. A message was then received stating that the Regiment was at that time a left flank guard to Buller's army, and that the former advance guard companies were to join the remainder of the Regiment.

The Boers, opposed to Buller in very considerable numbers, were sangared on some low hills about 800 yards distant from and in front of and below the high ridge over which his force had to advance. Buller made his dispositions behind this high ridge. The reverse slope was completely raked by the Boer fire, and no cover except that afforded by some ant-hills was obtainable. The dropping bullets

TREKKING WITH GENERAL BULLER
5-INCH GUNS ON THE MARCH

TREKKING WITH GENERAL BULLER
5-INCH GUNS ON THE MARCH

followed the form and slope of the hill, sothat neither front nor rear was secure.

As soon as the Regiment was formed up, an order was sent to advance. Captain Emerson with fifteen men extended, rushed down the forward slope under a heavy fire, and took cover behind some ant-hills. The moment the men showed over the crest line they were met by a hail of bullets, and further advance was impossible.

Later, another order was sent to advance, but owing to the want of cover it was found impossible for the line to make headway in the face of the fire brought to bear upon it. It was not until the Howitzer Battery was brought into action late in the day, to cover the retirement of the advanced companies, that Captain Emerson and his men were able to get back. This they did under a very heavy fire from rifles and machine guns.

One company under Lieutenant Harris, which had been moved off to the right, had advanced and got into an exposed place. The men took cover behind ant-hills, and remained there for the rest of the day. Three companies had been moved to the neighbourhood of the guns. These came under shell fire from the Boer guns and had some casualties, amongst whom was Colour-Sergeant Burchell, who was shot through the shoulder. Under General Buller's direct supervision one company was ordered forward. Immediately their four scouts showed over the crest line a storm of bullets met them, and they were all hit. The four scouts were found dead on the second day afterwards by the Liverpool Mounted Infantry.

Dusk found the companies posted as under: Three companies extended on the ridge on the left, with two companies extended in support on the rear side of the hill. One company was extended on the ridge in the centre, whilst three companies were near the guns, three-quarters of a mile away on the right. One man was killed and one wounded just at dark by unaimed fire and by the last shots fired. The companies on the ridge retired to the crest of the hill after dark and took up an entrenched outpost line for the night. Rations were then issued for the following day. It was a pitch-black night, and two cooks' orderlies who had gone to fetch their company's

A REGIMENT OF THE LINE

tea and sugar rations from their wagon, missed their way in the dark when returning, and walked into the Boer position, distant only a few hundred yards, and were made prisoners. These two men were the first prisoners of war lost to the battalion up to this date; and with the exception of one other prisoner, who was temporarily in the hands of the Boers in the Badfontein valley in the following year, they were the only men of the battalion taken prisoners during the war. The casualties of the battalion for the day were 6 killed, 15 wounded, and 2 prisoners.

Early the following morning the 7th Brigade, with the exception of the Manchester Regiment, moved off to the left, the Rifle Brigade, whose turn it was to lead, being in front. The guns accompanied the brigade.

There was little or no opposition till the scouts came under fire from Bergendal Kopje, or Drie Kraal as it was otherwise known. This rocky kopje was strongly fortified and held by the Boers. A Field Battery opened fire on to the kopje at about 3000 yards' range from some rising ground. Shortly afterwards the remaining guns—5-inch, 4·7's, naval

12-pounders, in all to the number of about thirty-nine—commenced pouring shells on to this one spot in the Boer position. This shelling continued for about three hours.

Very early in the morning a train had been seen coming out from Machadodorp with reinforcements. These, it was ascertained, were the Johannesburg Police, to the number of about eighty, and they formed the garrison of the kopje, about a hundred more being in the farm behind the kopje. This kopje was a small hill covered with large boulders. The rocks had been connected with large stones to form sangars, behind which the garrison found cover. A pompom was included in the armament of the position, which measured about eighty yards by forty yards only. It fell away abruptly in the rear, the farm and outbuildings lying very close under the steep rear side of the hill.

The English shells fell with terrible accuracy into the sangars, and there was an almost continuous explosion on the hill. Yet the Boers kept up their fire till the Rifle Brigade were within ten yards of them, and their pompom was in action, although partly jammed and

A REGIMENT OF THE LINE 129

firing single shots, till the very end. This pompom was bravely served by one man, the remainder of the gun team having been either killed or wounded. It is not known whether this plucky fellow survived or not.

General Walter Kitchener, who was commanding the infantry attack, decided to attack with the Rifle Brigade along the ridge which ended in the kopje, which was slightly above the level of the ridge. At the same time he ordered the Inniskilling Fusiliers to attack over the low ground on the Rifle Brigade's right, whilst the Gordon Highlanders and the Devonshire Regiment were held in support.

The Rifle Brigade started from the foot of the hills under which they had taken cover, and which was about 1200 yards from the Boer position, and almost immediately came under heavy musketry fire, being much exposed on the high open ridge.

They, however, continued their advance in perfect order and eventually rushed the kopje, the British shells dropping and the Boers firing till the assault had been delivered. The Inniskillings advanced across the low ground underneath the Rifle Brigade. Their advance was slightly delayed, and their delivery of the assault was consequently later than that of the Rifle Brigade. Captain Emerson with one company of the Regiment which had been told off as escort to the Maxim guns, advanced with the leading company of the Inniskillings.

The whole Boer position was evacuated as soon as their line had been penetrated by the capture of the Bergendal Kopje.

The casualties amongst the Rifle Brigade were severe, owing to the much exposed ground over which it was necessary for the attack to be delivered, and to the fact that, as the extended lines converged on to the small kopje, the men naturally became crowded and formed a better mark for the Boer rifles. They lost two officers and fourteen men killed and five officers and fifty men wounded, of whom two officers died of their wounds the following day. The Regiment had one man wounded.

The position was soon made good, although the Boers held on tenaciously to a long rocky ridge in their rear to which they had retired, till nightfall. The force bivouacked for the night near the farm.

This action was known officially as the battle of Belfast.

A quiet night was passed, and next morning, August 28th, the force occupied Machadodorp with slight opposition. The Boers were seen retreating up the road leading to Lydenburg, and on the high ground above the town they brought two big guns into action.

The Gordon Highlanders, in support of Dundonald's Mounted Brigade, were sent on through the town and occupied the high ground on the far side, and the Boers retired before them.

The Boers had made a very hurried retirement. In Machadodorp on the evening of the day of the fight, guns and cartloads of ammunition were parked in the big open space in the centre of the town. These were moved off very hurriedly on the approach of the British force, and the guns had only reached the top of the hills on the further side of Machadodorp when General Buller's infantry came in view. General Buller brought some long-range guns into action and shelled them as they ascended the hill, but without result.

From lack of efficient pursuit after the battle the evening before, and a too cautious advance in the morning, an opportunity to do the Boer forces considerable damage was apparently lost. A wagon containing pompom ammunition was captured by Dundonald's Mounted Brigade, but the pompom itself got away, notwithstanding the very slight opposition offered by the Boers.

The following day General Buller's forces reached Helvetia Farm, where General French's column and General Pole Carew's division joined up.

With the object of releasing the prisoners who had been sent by the Boers from Pretoria to Noitgedacht down the railway line towards Komati Poort, General Buller's force now turned eastwards and marched along the heights on the north side of the railway. On the first day out from Helvetia his cavalry saw some 2000 released English prisoners marching up the line towards Waterval Onder from the direction of Noitgedacht, and having been unable to obtain touch with the Boers, the force retraced their steps, and encamped some six miles from Helvetia at Vluchtfontein, and at this place a halt was made on the following day.

From here General Buller turned north, and on September 1st, advancing up the Lydenburg road, reached Badfontein on the Crocodile River. Here the army bivouacked for the night, and an advance was made up the Badfontein valley next morning, but coming into contact with the Boers who were holding the northern end of the valley, his further progress was checked. The Boer position extended along the high hills which straddled the road in a semicircular position some eight miles from Badfontein.

The Regiment formed the infantry advance guard of the army, and on reaching what was then named Redvers' Kopje and afterwards known as Devon Kopje, came under shell fire from three big guns which the Boers had brought into action on the hills above. At this place the Regiment stopped for the day, taking cover from shell fire behind the large boulders of rocks of which the kopje was composed. The remainder of Sir Redvers Buller's force returned to its old encampment of the previous night.

The two mounted brigades and one battery R.H.A., which had advanced to the foot of the hills occupied by the Boers, returned to camp at dusk.

As soon as it was dark, four companies of the Regiment were left on Devon Kopje as an advanced post, whilst the remainder of the Regiment retired to the rear of the hill and bivouacked. The kopje was entrenched and everything made comfortable for the following day. All the baggage wagons were sent back to the main camp during the night.

September 3rd, 4th, and 5th were spent quietly in position, the Boers on the 5th firing over the heads of the Regiment into the brigade camp, but doing very little damage. On the evening of the 5th a hill to the east was shelled, and after some opposition from the Boers, when Strathcona's Horse had some casualties, the hill was occupied by the 60th Rifles and the Leicester Regiment. A battery of artillery was then hauled up the steep incline to the top.

On the 6th, General Ian Hamilton having brought up reinforcements consisting of a brigade, from Belfast by way of Dullstrom,

A REGIMENT OF THE LINE 135

thus turning the Boers' right, General Buller advanced the following day and found that the Boers had evacuated their position. But, in ignorance of this retirement, great preparations were made for a big fight.

The Devonshire Regiment headed the advance of the infantry. It was divided into two half battalions, one half battalion under Major Davies proceeding up the road in support of the mounted troops, whilst five companies under Captain Jacson were sent more to the left to attack the large farm at the foot of the hill, with orders "to proceed as far as possible without severe loss." These manœuvres having been accomplished in safety without a shot being fired, the force reached the top and bivouacked some two miles further on for the night. Owing to the steepness of the road the baggage did not arrive till after midnight.

Lydenburg was occupied next day without opposition, the Boers having retired to a position on Paardeplaats, a range of high and irregular hills five miles distant from and overlooking Lydenburg on the Mauchberg-Spitzkop road. From this position the Boers shelled the baggage, bursting shrapnel over it as it defiled into the open in front of the town. The train formed up and halted under cover behind a hill, and came into camp at dusk.

The following morning, September 8th, Sir Redvers Buller decided to attack the Boer position on Paardeplaats, and for this purpose he detailed General Walter Kitchener's brigade to advance up the spurs of the hills against the Boers' right, whilst General Ian Hamilton's brigade was to turn the Boers' left, the attack being covered by the artillery which proceeded up the main road in the centre.

General Kitchener's brigade moved out from Lydenburg on to the race-course. The battalion being the leading regiment deployed and advanced towards a hill jutting out into the plain, with the mounted brigade of General Dundonald working round the left. This hill was afterwards known to the Regiment as Ben Tor. As the Regiment deployed into the open it came under shrapnel fire from two big guns posted on Paardeplaats. The Regiment was, however, extended, and had only one man wounded.

The Gordon Highlanders, who were in support, marched across the Boers' front, in rear of the extended Devons, in column of companies. Several shells burst amongst them, and one shell, bursting thirty feet above graze, took their volunteer company end on and killed and wounded fifteen.

With Dundonald's men on their left flank, four companies of the Regiment under Captain Jacson advanced up the spurs without opposition, whilst Major Davies, in command of the remaining companies, climbed the spurs on Jacson's right. Little or no opposition was met with on this flank. Jacson's companies were reinforced by four companies of the Gordon Highlanders and the 60th Rifles, and at 4 p.m., when nearing the summit, a thick mist came on, and the flanking brigade halted. Meanwhile Davies, with two of his companies, had reached the top of the hill and was proceeding down the far side when the fog lifted. It was then ascertained that the Boers, under cover of the fog, had left the position to which they had clung with great determination, and had retired. The position had been turned by Ian Hamilton's right flank attack.

The thick mist saved the Boers, who would otherwise undoubtedly have lost their big guns in their retirement.

Just before dark the companies of the Regiment, which had become scattered, were collected, and Captain Jacson received an order to return with these to the old camp on the far side of Lydenburg; seven companies were thus taken down the hills over very rough country to the old camp, a distance of nearly six miles. On arrival there a message was received which stated that the army was encamped half-way up the hill towards Paardeplaats. The seven companies then returned, and finally reached camp very late. They had been marching and climbing incessantly from 7.30 a.m. till 10 p.m.

The brigades had by this time become rather intermingled. Of General Kitchener's brigade the Manchester Regiment had been left behind at Witklip, at the north end of the Badfontein valley. A garrison had also been left at Lydenburg under General Howard, consisting of the Rifle Brigade and Leicesters, with General Brocklehurst's Cavalry Brigade.

The Devonshire Regiment was now left

A REGIMENT OF THE LINE 139

behind at Paardeplaats, while General Buller's force, consisting of the Gordon Highlanders and the 60th Rifles, with Dundonald's Mounted Brigade, two Field Batteries, and the 5-inch guns, advanced on the 9th, the day following the capture of Paardeplaats, in the direction of the Mauchberg.

The country was extremely difficult, and the Boer guns and pompoms well served, and considerable opposition was met with in the advance.

General Buller's force reached the Mauchberg that evening and proceeded on the following day to Devil's Knuckles, down the steep Mauchberg road (known as Hell's Gate), where the two Boer big guns again narrowly escaped capture, and so on to Spitzkop, just north of Nelspruit on the Pretoria-Lorenzo Marques railway.

On the 10th four companies and two guns under Captain Jacson were ordered to the Mauchberg. The companies got off by midday, and after a stiff climb occupied the mountain just before dark. The top of the Mauchberg, 8720 feet high, was found to be very extended, and the garrison was much split up. Company forts were erected on the main features, and the place was held till the 20th, mostly in thick fog and rain.

The Mauchberg post was the terminus of the telegraph line, communication thence with General Buller's head-quarters being continued by visual signalling. The mountain was intersected by deep kloofs and ravines, into most of which the Boers had collected their families and supplies, in the hope that neither would be found. These were all disclosed from the summit of the mountain, which commanded a view of a great extent of country. General Buller succeeded in collecting a large amount of stores from these "caches."

The families of Boers who surrendered with their stock were sent into Lydenburg, together with any prisoners that had been taken.

On the 11th two of the Mauchberg companies with the two guns were ordered to proceed to Devil's Knuckles, to supply picquets for Dundonald's Mounted Brigade which was stationed there, and on September 20th the companies of the Regiment stationed at Paardeplaats marched to the Mauchberg,

DEVONS CROSSING THE SABI RIVER

A REGIMENT OF THE LINE

being relieved at the former place by the Leicesters, the remaining two Mauchberg companies proceeding to Devil's Knuckles.

On the 21st the Regiment was again united and marched with Dundonald's Brigade down the Sabi Valley, reaching Sabi Drift that evening, where the force bivouacked. The column under General Dundonald remained at Sabi Drift till the 26th awaiting the arrival of General Buller, who was returning from Spitzkop.

A story is told anent the positions out of which General Buller's infantry had turned the Boers, which goes to show the estimation in which the British infantry were held by their opponents. The words are those of General Botha, and were told to an officer of the Headquarter Staff. "I shall give it up," he said. "I have taken up position after position which I considered impregnable; I have always been turned off by your infantry, who come along in great lines in their dirty clothes with bags on their backs. Nothing can stop them. I shall give it up."

On September 25th the remainder of General Buller's force marched into Sabi

Drift, and on the 26th the army, united again, advanced north for Pilgrim's Rest. Burgher's Nek and Mac-Mac diggings were reached about noon on that day.

The pass over Burgher's Nek was held by the Boers under Gravett, Botha and the State treasure with a small escort having crossed only a few hours before, whilst a portion of their army under Viljoen retired at the same time to the north towards Pietersburg.

The infantry of the advance guard was composed of four companies of the Regiment under Captain Jacson. On reaching the foot of the pass the mounted troops were checked and the artillery came into action. The position occupied by the Boers was formidable—a long stretch of high rugged hills, with the forward slope ending precipitously. The pass lay over a Nek between two high shoulders of hills. The Boers, exceedingly well posted, occupied the hills on either side of the Nek, taking cover behind the immense boulders on the summit.

After the artillery had been bombarding the south side of the Nek for some considerable time, the mounted infantry were sent forward to occupy the hill known as Grass Kop, but were unable to proceed. In the meantime, the four companies of the advance guard had been moved off to the left and nearer to the hills. They now got the order to attack and occupy the hill. Whilst these companies moved off under cover of the undulating ground to the foot of the hills, two companies with the Maxim gun took up a position in rear to cover the advance, firing with a range of 1700 yards at the top of the hill. Most of the artillery came into action at the same time and at the same objective. The foot of the hill was reached by the attacking force with two casualties. One company was then directed to the left to attack round the flank, and the ascent of the precipitous side of the hill was commenced. Crawling up a goat's track in single file, on hands and knees, through dense bush, the first portion of the ascent was accomplished, and the little force formed up under a spur to get breath before debouching into the open for the final rush to the top. After a short halt the advance was continued to the summit, the companies on their way coming under a smart shell fire from their own guns (happily without casualties), which were bursting shrapnel with wonderful precision between the two leading companies. Just before reaching the top the flanking company, coming in from the left with a well-timed advance, joined the general advance to the summit. It was found that the Boers had retired, and fire was brought to bear on them as they descended the rear slope of the hill. The high hill on the left of the pass was then occupied, and the Nek over which the road passed cleared of Boers.

A heliograph message from Sir Redvers Buller was received on the summit, "Well done Devons!" and in Lord Roberts' official dispatch for the day it was notified that General Buller had occupied Burgher's Nek, and that "the pass had been turned by a half battalion of the Devonshire Regiment, well led by Captain Jacson."

The four companies bivouacked on the top. Efforts were made by those down below to get food and blankets up to them, but owing to the steepness and difficulties of the climb and the darkness, it was found impossible.

The head-quarter companies of the Regiment were engaged on outpost duty at the foot of the pass, where the army had bivouacked, almost all the men being on duty.

On the following day the march was resumed, the head-quarter companies of the Regiment being rear-guard to the force. The companies on the hill were relieved by two companies of the Regiment under Captain Wren. The road was extremely bad and crossed by many drifts, which caused considerable delay, and it was not till the early hours of morning that the rear-guard companies got into camp. The bivouac was formed amongst the hills, some five miles from Pilgrim's Rest, which had been occupied the previous day by Strathcona's Horse.

On the 28th the march was continued through Pilgrim's Rest to the foot of Morgenzon Hill, the mounted troops surprising the Boers on the summit and putting them to flight.

The baggage was safely brought up the six miles of steep hill on the following day. The road, which was the old coaching highway Pilgrim's Rest-Lydenburg, was found in excellent condition, but it was heavy work for the oxen, and all wagons were double spanned. The force camped on the summit, and halted there on the 30th.

A good number of Boers were reported in the vicinity to the west and north, but they did not make their presence felt and Sunday was spent quietly.

On October 1st Morgenzon was left and the march continued towards Kruger's Post and Lydenburg. It was a long, dusty road through narrow valleys. Opposition was encountered at the bifurcation of the Lydenburg-Morgenzon and Lydenburg-Ohrigstadt roads, which, however, was soon overcome, the Boers retiring to the hills out of reach of the guns, and Kruger's Post was reached at 2 p.m.

Shortly after the Regiment had settled itself in its bivouac a Boer big gun opened on to it from a hill about 6000 yards distant, and not very far from the road. This gun also shelled the wagons as they came into camp, necessitating their halting under cover and coming in later. In the evening, about 6.30, the Boers brought another gun into action on a hill due west of the camp, and shelled the cavalry and infantry bivouacs for one and a half hours in the dark. After several shells had pitched into their midst the Regiment moved out and formed up into two long lines and entrenched.

It was whilst marching out to take up this position in the dark that a shell emptied itself into the head of one company, killing Lieutenant Cumin and severely wounding Captain Luxmoore and one man. The South African Light Horse and Strathcona's Horse had a number of casualties amongst their men and horses.

The Boers by a skilful manœuvre had kept their guns concealed, ready to be brought into action as soon as General Buller's army had settled itself quietly in its bivouac. They expended some cartloads of ammunition in this manner without interference. In the early hours of the following morning a band of volunteers ascended the hill to capture the guns. They had both been withdrawn and were not traced.

On the morning of October 2nd Buller's army reached Lydenburg without further opposition. Lieutenant Cumin was buried in the evening in Lydenburg cemetery.

On Saturday, October 6th, Sir Redvers Buller bade farewell to his army. The troops lined the streets and roads and gave him a hearty send-off. He was immensely popular with the men and they were sorry to see him go.

General W. Kitchener took over command of the Lydenburg district and its garrison, on Sir Redvers Buller's departure.

On the writer asking Sir Redvers on the eve of the day of his departure which was his best army—the one he commanded into Ladysmith or the one with which he trekked north—he replied, "The army I went north with was the best. I watched the Devons pass me at Burgher's Nek and it struck me how wonderfully well they looked. I considered they were ready for anything I asked them to do; but," he added, "they surprised me with the pace they went up the hill at Burgher's Nek."

COLONEL C. W. PARK
MISSION CAMP, LYDENBURG

CHAPTER IV

LYDENBURG

1900-1901

ON October 8th, 1900, the battalion moved out of Lydenburg to the Mission Station, three miles north of the town on the Kruger's Post road. The Mission Station was a collection of Kaffir houses, containing some 500 Christian men, women, and children. The mission-house was taken over as a post and fortified as soon as the German pastor, who was found to be communicating with the Boers, had been sent to Pretoria to be locked up.

The site of the camp having been chosen, it was immediately surrounded by company forts consisting of ditches four feet deep and two feet wide for protection against shell fire, which it was considered possible would be brought to bear on the camp. This entrenchment was finished in one afternoon.

Two guns of the 53rd Battery under Lieutenant Higgins, and one 5-inch gun under Second Lieutenant McLellan, were added to the garrison.

The battalion stood to arms daily just before dawn.

On the 9th two companies under Captain Bartlett were moved to Paardeplaats as a permanent garrison, whilst two companies under Captain Travers were sent to Ben Tor.

On the 10th two companies of the Regiment, two guns, and one company mounted infantry proceeded just before daylight to a farm some six miles away, and burnt it. They encountered no opposition. This company of mounted infantry was then added to the garrison for permanent duty.

The two following days were employed in collecting forage from different farm-houses. Very few Boers were seen, and there was little or no opposition.

On the 24th, it having been ordained that all the Boer women in the various towns were to be sent out to their husbands in the laagers, two companies and two guns under Captain Ravenshaw were ordered to escort the ladies of Lydenburg over the Spekboom Bridge on the Kruger's Post road, and there hand them over to their husbands and friends. Captain Ravenshaw went out with a flag of truce and met the Boers, amongst whom was Erasmus. They were most affable, and shook hands cordially. The women reached Kruger's Post that evening.

The next day General Walter Kitchener started out at 2 a.m. with a column of infantry (Devons), mounted infantry and guns towards Kruger's Post for the purpose of shelling the farm. At dawn the column crossed the Spekboom Bridge and mounted the hills in the face of slight opposition. A 5-inch gun was then brought to the front and shells dropped into Kruger's Post, after which the column returned to camp. A patrol of four Boers was captured, and there were no casualties on the British side.

Very shortly after this the order concerning the Boer women was cancelled and a fresh order was issued, which ordained that all Boer women who were captured or gave themselves up should be confined in large concentration camps on the railway line.

On the evening of the 24th one company was ordered down from Ben Tor to be posted on the hill overlooking the Spekboom Bridge. The company proceeded there on the 25th escorted by two companies, two guns, and some mounted infantry.

On the following day, as the Boers were threatening the Bridge Post before the works were complete, one company and two guns were sent out as a covering party.

The battalion was now split up; two companies under Lieutenant Tringham proceeded to Witklip, two companies under Captain Bartlett were at Paardeplaats, one company under Lieutenant Cowie was at Ben Tor, one company under Captain Travers was at Bridge Post. Of the three remaining companies one was holding the Mission House, and the two others with the 5-inch gun and the two field guns formed the garrison of the main camp.

On October 30th two companies from Mission Camp were ordered to march at sunset through Lydenburg to the bank of the river. Here they halted and had supper, being eventually joined by the Rifle Brigade. Starting again at 9 p.m. and marching all through the night, they attacked some Boer laagers at dawn. After some heavy firing the laagers, which had been completely surprised, were captured with all their tents, etc. The column returned at 5 p.m. the same day, when the companies redistributed themselves to their various posts, having marched from 4 a.m. till 10.30 p.m. a distance of thirty-five miles. There were four casualties, one of which was a Devon man slightly wounded.

November was spent rather quietly by the battalion, the men being employed in strengthening the various posts and making them comfortable.

On November 7th one company was sent off to garrison Strathcona Hill on the southern side of the town.

On the 8th General Walter Kitchener again attacked the Boers, this time employing entirely mounted troops. He brought back with him 1000 sheep, 50 ponies, and 20 wagons. Five Boers were killed, and the mounted troops had two casualties.

Colonel Park returned from sick leave on

the 9th, when Major Davies resumed his position as second in command. Lieutenants Hext and Kane left shortly afterwards to join the mounted infantry at Pretoria, and at the end of November Lieutenant Woollcombe rejoined the Regiment from Maritzburg, Lieutenant Harris returned from Pretoria with a draft of thirty-eight men, and Lieutenant Twiss rejoined from hospital at Newcastle.

At the beginning of December the following was the distribution of the companies of the Regiment :—

Two companies at Paardeplaats under Captain Bartlett.

One company at Ben Tor under Lieutenant Cowie.

One company at Bridge Post under Captain Travers.

One company at Strathcona Hill under Lieutenant Willis ; and

Four companies at Mission Camp.

On December 9th and 10th a foraging expedition with three guns and four companies of the Rifle Brigade went out towards Van Der Merves' Farm under Colonel Park. These brought back twenty-eight wagon loads of forage without experiencing any opposition.

It was reported on the 12th that Nelspruit had been cut off by the Boers and required assistance. A column was immediately formed, composed of one squadron 19th Hussars, four companies Devons under Major Davies, and four companies Rifle Brigade with some guns; the whole proceeding under General Kitchener *en route* to the Mauchberg and Devil's Knuckles. Three companies of the Regiment had been taken from Mission Camp and one from Paardeplaats.

A blizzard blowing all night and the following morning, accompanied with thunder and heavy rain, delayed the advance of the troops till noon, when a start was effected, and the Mauchberg was occupied by the Devons without opposition.

Further advance down Hell's Gate to the Devil's Knuckles was found impracticable owing to the state of the road. Troops from Machadodorp had been sent to Lydenburg to act as a garrison whilst the column was out; but instructions were received from headquarters on the 15th ordering the immediate return of the column to Lydenburg, as well as of the reinforcements back to Machadodorp. The Devons had been, however, sent out from the Mauchberg previous to the receipt of the order to retire. They skirmished down the road towards Devil's Knuckles, and in a very thick fog Boers and British nearly walked into each other's arms. There was a good deal of musketry fire, with the result to the British side of one Devon wounded. As was usually said on such occasions, "Boers' loss was probably very great." The three companies returned to Mission Camp late on the evening of the 16th.

On the 18th Major Davies was ordered to Witklip to take command of the forts; he took with him one company as a reinforcement to the garrison.

On Christmas Day the Regiment received a number of telegrams from friends in England wishing them good luck. A race meeting was held in the afternoon on the Lydenburg race-course. The public went armed, and two field guns were brought into action on the course. These precautions were necessary, for the Boers at this time were very

A REGIMENT OF THE LINE 157

busy, and on the night of December 28th–29th attacked the post at Helvetia, near Machadodorp, and captured it.

The post contained a 4·7 naval gun called "Lady Roberts," and this, with the garrison of three companies of the Liverpool Regiment, was taken, only one small fort manned by a small contingent of about fifteen men holding out. General Walter Kitchener left at once with four companies of the Rifle Brigade, two companies of the Regiment (from Witklip), two guns, and the mounted troops, in the hope of intercepting the Boers and recovering the gun. The Boers, however, had made good their retirement to the hills, and General Kitchener returned to Lydenburg with the column on the 31st.

The Liverpool Regiment lost at Helvetia 4 killed, 27 wounded, and 200 prisoners.

The Boers about this time attacked all along the line from Lydenburg to Pretoria. The defences, except at Lydenburg, were of the most meagre description. In fact, the works constructed by the Rifle Brigade and the Devons at Lydenburg were the only works of any strength, and these were as complete as possible. Witklip was being placed in a fortified condition, but up to the time of the taking of Helvetia Post little had been done anywhere, except at Lydenburg.

For the next few nights all posts round Lydenburg stood to arms at 1.30 a.m. owing to the activity of the Boers, but it was not till January 4th that they attacked the Bridge Hill Post. They attempted to capture the picquet on the bridge over the Spekboom River, but were beaten off.

About this time one company was ordered down from Paardeplaats to Mission Camp, the garrison at Paardeplaats being thus reduced to one company; and Witklip garrison was reinforced by the addition of one company, which was sent there from Mission Camp.

On the early morning of January 8th the Boers made a simultaneous attack on almost all posts on the line between Belfast and Lydenburg. The following posts were attacked: Badfontein, Schwarzkop, Helvetia, Machadodorp, Belfast, Pan, and Noitgedacht. The Badfontein Post was shelled only, by a big gun mounted on the hills west of the fort,

A REGIMENT OF THE LINE 159

which failed, however, to reach the post. The result of the general attack was that two posts only, those at Belfast, were captured by the Boers. These were not held, and the Boers retired, leaving twenty-four dead upon the ground. The posts had been well prepared for defence after the disaster at Helvetia.

A wire bridge over the Lydenburg River, constructed by Lieutenant Green and the twelve men of the Maxim gun team, was completed about this time, and as it attracted a good deal of attention a description of it may be interesting.

The bridge had a span of sixty feet, and was constructed on the system of the "jhula," or rope bridge, of Cashmere, out of telegraph wire. The roadway, to admit of one person at a time, was made of two lengths of twisted wire, each ten strands thick. These being stretched tightly across the river, and the ends well worked into the ground and pegged down, were joined together by small laths of wood two inches apart. Two more lengths, each ten strands thick, were stretched from two uprights on each bank, at a convenient height above the roadway, to form a support for it. These were joined on to the roadway by stout sticks, about one to two feet apart, on either side to give stability. The bridge was then secured up and down stream by wires to keep it steady. The height of the bridge above the stream was about twenty feet.

The chief cause of attraction and interest in the bridge to outsiders was the fact that it had been constructed entirely by British infantry without the aid of the Royal Engineers, and that the plan had been thought out by them alone, and was not " in the book." The idea had been taken from some photographs of a Cashmere "jhula," and the work had been carried out from descriptions of the rope bridges furnished by an officer of the Regiment who had crossed them. All previous bridges had been washed away, but this bridge was still standing at the end of the war, and was being utilized then by the Kaffirs at Mission Camp as an easy access and short cut to their cultivated fields.

On January 12th, as a larger convoy than usual was coming through to Lydenburg, a small force under Captain Jacson, consisting of two companies Devons, one company

WIRE BRIDGE, LYDENBURG　　　　Page 158

WIRE BRIDGE, LYDENBURG
(GENERAL KITCHENER AND COLONEL PARK)　　　　Page 160

mounted infantry and one gun went out from Mission Camp to demonstrate towards Schoeman's Laager on the west. No Boers, however, were seen, and the convoy came safely into Lydenburg without opposition.

Several changes occurred in the disposition of the companies of the Regiment during the latter half of January, 1901.

The head-quarters with three companies were stationed at Witklip under Colonel Park. Two companies proceeded to Badfontein as a garrison under Major Davies. One company held each of the posts at Bridge Hill and Paardeplaats respectively. One company was in charge of the Mission House, whilst one company was left at Mission Camp to commence the construction of a new work south of the old camp.

These changes were made on account of some large convoys going and coming to and from the railway line, larger escorts having to be provided owing to the proximity and increased activity of the Boers on the lines of communication. The convoys came through safely without any trouble, and on January 30th Major Davies with his two companies returned to Witklip. The head-quarters of the Regiment, with three companies, left Witklip the following day and proceeded to Mission Camp. Further changes were made during February, 1901, the post at Paardeplaats being given up and the company posted there returning to Mission Camp.

Towards the latter end of January a flying column was organized by General Walter Kitchener. The objective of this column was the high hills south of Lydenburg towards Witpoort and Belfast. It was under the personal command of the General, and was composed of the following troops :—

1 squadron 19th Hussars.
1 battery R.F.A.
1 naval 12-pounder.
1 pompom.
1 company Manchester Mounted Infantry.
3 companies Devons under Captain Travers.

The column set out at 1 a.m. in the direction of Elandskloof. It was a bright night, although a thick white mist hung everywhere. The 19th Hussars, who knew the difficult country, conducted the advance. After marching for two hours the column found itself in the hills. A halt was made whilst the three companies of the Regiment extended and occupied the high ground which barred the advance, to drive off any Boers who might be in possession. This manœuvre was executed without opposition. It was learnt, however, that a Boer picquet had been on the top, and had galloped off on the approach of the infantry. Daylight found the column in possession of Elandskloof, which was reached after a difficult climb by steep and circuitous paths. Shortly after daylight several Boers were observed to be driving their cattle into kloofs above the Badfontein valley for safety. An advance was made shortly afterwards towards Schwartz Kopjes, which place was reached without much opposition towards dark. At Schwartz Kopjes camp was formed for the night, the infantry entrenching themselves in the kopjes round the camp, with one company posted in a farmhouse about 400 yards west of the main camp.

On the following day General Kitchener ordered the mounted troops and guns to make a reconnaissance towards Dulstroom. Whilst the rest of the force remained in camp, the baggage under escort was sent towards Belfast. The reconnoitring force fared badly, for after advancing a few miles Boers in large numbers were seen collecting on the high hills due west, and approaching at a rapid pace. The reconnoitring force was shortly afterwards heavily engaged, and compelled to retire on to the camp.

The infantry were now ordered to retire as rapidly as possible to a ridge in rear, distant about 2000 to 2500 yards. The cavalry retired hard pressed on to Schwartz Kopjes, which they held until the infantry had completed their movement, when the cavalry again retired back to the neighbourhood of the infantry. Schwartz kopjes were immediately occupied by the Boers, who collected there in large numbers and endeavoured to get round the flanks of the column.

Followed hotly by the Boers, the column made a rapid retirement, units covering each other until camp was reached. It was only then that the Boers drew off. There was no further engagement that day or during the night, and the column completed its advance

A REGIMENT OF THE LINE 165

next day to Belfast, where it arrived about midday and camped to the south side of the railway.

The distribution of the garrison, carried out at the commencement of February, continued more or less the same till the time the Regiment left Lydenburg. Three companies were north of Lydenburg, and were stationed at the Mission House, Mission Camp Fort, and Bridge Hill. One company was at Strathcona Hill, south of the town, two companies under the command of Major Davies were at Witklip, whilst the three companies which had proceeded with General Kitchener to Belfast were quartered on their return in Lydenburg.

During this time Colonel Park was commanding the Lydenburg district with Captain Ravenshaw as Brigade Major.

On February 5th the Boers attacked all the Lydenburg posts. The attacks were not heavily pressed. There were no casualties on the side of the defenders, whilst the Boers lost, as far as could be ascertained, two killed and seven wounded.

On February 16th two Boers surrendered

at Mission Camp. These stated that their friends in the laagers were badly off for meat and had hardly any horses left, most of them having died of horse-sickness.

Early in March, 1901, Colonel Park decided on raiding Piet Schwartz's laager, which was stationed on the ridge to the north of and overlooking Kruger's Post. His force consisted of three companies Devons under Captain Jacson, three companies Rifle Brigade, three companies Royal Irish, one squadron 19th Hussars, three companies mounted infantry, three guns 53rd Battery, one howitzer, and one pompom, and by the 12th his arrangements were complete. The infantry were to make a night march and to attack at dawn, whilst the mounted troops and guns were to be at Kruger's Post just after dawn to assist.

Under cover of darkness, the column rendezvoused at the Spekboom Bridge, one company having gone on ahead to seize any Boers who might be coming down at nightfall, as was their wont, to form a picquet there.

A start was made from the bridge at about 9 p.m. Leaving the main road on their left, the column proceeded in single file, Devons leading, along a footpath which led them over a Nek in the hills and thence down into a donga. An accident, which might have been attended with very unfortunate results, occurred at the very commencement. The Royal Irish, who were in the rear, instead of following and keeping in touch with the remainder of the column missed connection, and went up the main road, on which, about two miles ahead, was a Boer picquet. They were, however, stopped just in time and turned back. This delayed the advance for about an hour. Along the donga the march was continued for some six miles, when a cross donga was met with, the sides of which were steep and about fifteen feet high. The leading troops crossed and halted on the far side till the rear closed up. The Maxim gun mules with difficulty negotiated the obstacle, and the advance was, after one hour's halt, continued to Kruger's Post.

The force kept to the donga almost the whole march, scarcely for a moment leaving its shelter. Terribly rough going it was, with long high grass soaking wet, and the men tumbling about into ruts and over rocks. On they trudged, twisting and turning, up and down, falling about, with every now and then a suppressed exclamation and an imprecation on rocks and ruts in general and night marches in particular—no lights, no smoking. No one except he who has done it knows what a strain it is marching along through the dark night, without a word and without the company of a pipe.

On emerging from the donga at Kruger's Post on to the open veldt a further halt was made; the leading troops lay down in the soaking grass and were fast asleep in a moment.

It was found that the column had opened out considerably, and must have stretched for some four miles from lead to end. The rate of marching at the head of the column had been about two miles per hour. This was found, over the rough ground, to be too quick to allow of the rear keeping closed up—the pace should not have exceeded one mile an hour.

The column having closed up and the sleeping men having with difficulty been found and turned up out of the wet grass, a further

A REGIMENT OF THE LINE

advance was made. But now the direction was to the right in order to avoid Kruger's Post Farm, which was occupied by the Boers. This took the column over some millraces, a biggish jump for the men. The mules, having been relieved of their loads, were man-handled across. Once over these and then a wade through a stream knee deep, the ghostly column again halted. It was now 3.30 a.m. The foot of the low hills behind which was the laager, had been reached, and the officers were busy getting their men collected.

An intelligence officer reports that if there is the slightest delay dawn will break before the positions are reached. The first streak of dawn is 4.45 a.m.

"May we go off now on our own?" is the question asked.

"All right; off you go!" is the cheery answer from Colonel Park.

The Devons had the furthest to go, perhaps one and a half miles to reach the far side of the laager. The Royal Irish were already at the foot of the hill on the top of which was the position assigned to them.

Two of the Rifle Brigade companies had

unfortunately missed connection and had gone off into the "Ewigkeit" in the dark, but one company was ready and handy to the Nek which they had to occupy, to fill up the gap between the Devons and the Royal Irish.

The Devons, who by this time were well together, started off, Captain Travers with a guide leading. He had orders to take on with him the two first companies, the guide showing him where to place his men. On they went, running and walking, walking and running, up the slippery road, across the Nek and then down into the valley below. Two small groups of men were posted in the ditch leading up to the Nek.

As the last man reached the knoll overlooking the Nek at the place where the main road crossed it, and which was the right of the Devons' allotment of position, the two leading companies could be heard down in the valley below stumbling amongst the stones, getting into a position that would entirely cut off the Boers' retreat down the main road leading north.

Suddenly all was still: everything was ready. It was exactly 4.45 a.m.

MISSION CAMP FORT, LYDENBURG

MISSION CAMP FORT, LYDENBURG
(INTERIOR)

All lay down and waited in breathless silence for the coming dawn. The Devons had orders to withhold their fire as long as possible, to make sure of the other units being in their places. "That's the position of the laager, just behind that little knoll," whispered an intelligence scout; "but it seems as if the bird has flown."

For some ten minutes the silence continued, with not so much as the crack of a twig to interrupt it. What's that? It's a cock crowing! There it is again! There's another! The laager's there right enough, and we've got them!

In the far distance, Lydenburg way, the faint noise of musketry fire could be heard; it was the mounted troops advancing and driving in the Boer picquets on the road above the Spekboom Bridge, eight miles back.

In about five minutes' time the laager was roused by a Boer, who commenced swearing roundly at some one in a very loud voice. One man came out and posted himself on a little rise of ground, and gazed, listening, Kruger's Post way. He was joined by another, then another, until there was a group of nine of them, two dressed in long white robes. It was thought that these were women. Suddenly they all returned into the laager out of sight, only to appear again in a few minutes on horseback. Three of them came straight up to the high road just under the knoll where the Devons were in readiness. They were allowed to go on, and they continued their career down the road towards Kruger's Post.

Now the utility of posting the groups in the ditch by the side of the road became manifest. Suddenly from their direction crack ! went a single rifle, then a burst of rifle fire, which was immediately taken up all round the circle.

No, not quite round ; there was silence from the hill which should have been occupied by the Royal Irish. A party of some twenty Boers were seen ascending this hill, the top of which was covered with big rocks. The Devons' rifles as well as their Maxim gun were turned on to them. The Boers, however, succeeded in reaching the safety of the rocks a few moments before the ascending Irish.

Meanwhile the firing had become general, and in the dim light also a trifle mixed. The

A REGIMENT OF THE LINE

Rifle Brigade fired into the two Devon companies down in the valley and across the laager. The latter in their turn fired at some Boers trying to escape through the gap left open by the Royal Irish. These were striving with the Boers for the possession of the rock-capped hill, and both were being fired into by the Devons across the valley.

After some twenty minutes of sharp musketry fire the "cease fire" sounded, and everything was again quiet; it was then found that the whole laager had fallen into British hands. Two Boers were killed, three wounded, and thirty-six captured, whilst the British casualties were two killed and four wounded, all of them Royal Irish.

The distance from Lydenburg to Piet Schwartz's laager by road is about eighteen miles; the distance marched by the column could not have been under twenty miles, and this over very difficult ground. The column had left Lydenburg at 7 p.m., and reached its destination at 4.45 a.m.

Unfortunately, Piet Schwartz himself escaped capture, as he was not in the laager; he had left it the previous day.

The mounted troops and guns were very slow in coming out, with the result that a large quantity of cattle located in the various kloofs which should have been captured, escaped. Abel Erasmus was taken the following day.

The force bivouacked at Kruger's Post for the night, and returned to Lydenburg next day, bringing with it fifteen Boer families in addition to the prisoners. On their return a wire was received by Colonel Park from Lord Kitchener : " Highly appreciate successful operation of Colonel Park and troops engaged."

The remainder of the month was spent mostly in convoy work between Witklip and Lydenburg. Whilst returning to Lydenburg with one of these convoys, General Walter Kitchener, who was riding ahead with a small escort, suddenly came across some Boers lying concealed in the grass. He lost two of his own personal escort killed, his own horse also being shot. He himself narrowly escaped capture.

On April 10th an order was issued for the battalion to concentrate in Lydenburg, preparatory to a general advance of three columns. The posts at Bridge Hill, Mission Village, Strathcona, and Paardeplaats were evacuated, and the company at Witklip withdrawn.

The destinations of the columns were as follows:—

One column under Colonel Park was to proceed in the Kruger's Post direction and to scour the country towards the north, and later to join hands with General Kitchener's column, which was to proceed in a north-westerly direction, and the third column under Colonel Douglas was to proceed from Witklip in a westerly direction.

On the 12th, Lieutenant-Colonel Park handed over the command of the battalion to Major Davies, who had arrived from Witklip, and Captain Jacson took over the duties of second in command.

CHAPTER V

TREKKING IN THE NORTH-EAST TRANSVAAL

ON April 13th, 1901, General Walter Kitchener commenced his long trek with a night march.

His force consisted of—

Two guns 53rd F.B.R.A. under Major Johnson and Captain Talbot-Ponsonby.
One 5-inch gun.
One 5-inch howitzer.
One naval 12-pounder.
One company mounted infantry.
1st Battalion Devonshire Regiment (20 officers and 900 men).
2nd Battalion Rifle Brigade.
The 6th Western Australians.

General Walter Kitchener's column formed one of the many operating at the time in a

A REGIMENT OF THE LINE

combined movement in the Northern Transvaal and bush veldt, under the direction of General Sir Bindon Blood.

Two columns were sent north to drive the bush veldt, forcing any Boers that might be located there on to the other columns, who were acting as stops near the Tautes Berg and Bothas Berg, immediately north of the Pretoria-Lorenzo railway line.

General Walter Kitchener decided to start his operations with an attack on Schoeman's laager, and for this purpose the Regiment was ordered to take up a position before dawn which would cut off the laager, situated in the Steenkampsberg mountains, near the entrance of the Lydenburg road into the hills, from the north. This entailed a night march of about sixteen miles. The remainder of the column was to proceed by the main road and attack the laager at daybreak.

The Regiment rendezvoused on the west side of the river, clear of the town, before dusk. Here the men had food, and a start was made at 7 p.m. The going at first was fairly simple, but once the track was left the ground became rough, stony, and intersected with dongas. The advance was then made in single file.

As an instance of how a small obstruction delays troops marching in the dark, one small water-course 1½ feet wide and about 1 foot deep delayed the head of the column for some thirty-five minutes, till all the men had crossed and were closed up again, and then in crossing one in every ten fell into it. The top of the Steenkampsberg was reached at about 1 a.m., after a steep climb over a rough track. The difficulty of the march was increased by a thick fog. On the far side a steep cliff, at the bottom of which was a deep donga and a mountain torrent, was encountered, and this had to be negotiated on hands and knees. Slipping and sliding down, the bottom of the donga was reached and the mountain torrent waded, and then after a steep ascent the top of the plateau was reached.

It was here that the laager was supposed to be situated, and an extension was made and the advance continued. Just as the dawn was breaking some flying Boers, appearing and disappearing in the fog, were fired at by the leading extended company. The Boers had been disturbed prematurely and had escaped, taking with them their pompom, but the wagon containing its ammunition fell into the hands of the Regiment.

The actual position of the laager was found to be about one mile away from where it had been previously located, and was very difficult to find in the dark owing to the undulations of the ground at the top of the ridge. Complete success under these circumstances was scarcely probable, but as a test as to what a regiment could do when called upon, the undertaking was effective and complete.

After the Regiment had been engaged in long-range firing for some time, the head of the main column appeared on the Lydenburg road, and the force finally went into bivouac for the night at Boshhoek. About 400 sheep and some cattle were picked up on the neighbouring farms.

The following morning the column marched north down the Waterval valley, and after the mounted troops had experienced some opposition in very hilly and rough country, Boshfontein was reached.

Shortly after the force had settled into

camp heavy gun fire was heard from the direction of Waterval. The Boers' shells exploded in the valley immediately to the north of the camp and in the vicinity of a farm, where it would appear the Boers considered the column should have bivouacked. After the explosion of some twenty shells a louder report than usual was heard, and the shelling ceased.

The mounted troops reported that the Boers were in position above Waterval, where there was a large women's laager.

In the dark of the morning, at three o'clock, General Kitchener set his column in motion: four companies, with a 12-pounder and two 5-inch guns, under Major Davies, preceded the force, with the intention of capturing the big Boer gun; four companies, with two field guns, under Captain Jacson, made a flanking movement through scrub and dongas round the left. Very little opposition was met with. The mounted troops captured a few prisoners, and it was found that the Boers had blown up their big gun. This was the gun that had been situated on Pepworth Hill, and which had been disabled by one of the Naval Brigade's shells during the siege of Ladysmith. Its

REMAINS OF BOER BIG GUN, WATERVAL

A REGIMENT OF THE LINE

muzzle had been shortened, showing that it had been damaged. The Boers had blown the gun to pieces. The barrel of the gun was blown about fifty yards in front of the emplacement, whilst the breech-block was found afterwards $1\frac{1}{2}$ miles in rear. They had destroyed also one pompom and one Maxim. Twenty-eight Boers were captured, with about sixty head of cattle and thirteen wagons. The Australians had one man killed and one man wounded.

The Waterval valley was well watered and exceedingly rich in crops, and the numerous farm-houses were full of families. These were collected afterwards by Colonel Park's column and sent into Lydenburg.

On the 16th the column set out from Waterval in a north-westerly direction, the objective being Secoconi's country and Magnet Heights. The first day found the force on the east bank of the Steelpoort River. The Dwars River, which was found in full flood owing to a very violent thunderstorm, had been forded on the way. The Regiment was rear-guard to the column, and, owing to delay in passing the baggage over the river, reached camp some considerable time after dark. The Australian mounted troops did not halt at the Steelpoort, but, fording the river, pushed on to Magnet Heights, which they occupied the same night. Park's column had been in touch with Kitchener's in the morning.

On the banks of the Dwars River Secoconi's men were first met with. These, armed with rifles of various patterns ancient and modern, were out scouting for General Kitchener in all directions.

At dawn on April 17th the crossing of the Steelpoort River was commenced. One company of the Regiment was first sent across to occupy the high ground on the far side and to cover the crossing. The river was in flood owing to the heavy rain of the previous day, and the water above the men's waist. The advanced company having got safely across and having occupied the high ground, the remainder of the infantry were sent over without casualty. The march was then continued towards Magnet Heights, which was reached at dusk. Here camp was formed, and on the following day the march was again resumed with mule transport only, through Secoconi's land.

CROSSING THE STEELPORT RIVER

A REGIMENT OF THE LINE 183

Secoconi was at the time at war with a neighbouring tribe, and a fringe of hills only, divided the combatant parties, but an interval was called in their operations by mutual consent to allow of the passage of the British through their respective countries. On leaving behind the outposts of one, the outposts of the other were met with.

Having reached this point to the north of the Transvaal, General Kitchener's column was in a position to turn south, and, in conjunction with other columns on his right and left hand, to sweep the bush veldt and mountains southward towards the railway, near which another force under the personal command of Sir Bindon Blood, who was in charge of the entire operations, was drawn up ready to intercept any Boers who might try to move across the railway from north to south.

At Vergelegen, where the column halted for the night of the 18th, some of Secoconi's headmen came into camp for an interview. They were much impressed with what they saw, patted the 5-inch gun with friendly concern, and having relieved the General of his tobacco-pouch and a box of cigars, and offering their assistance when not busy with their neighbours, returned to their kraals.

The mounted troops were sent on ahead the same day to Pokwani town, where it was supposed the Boers had collected a quantity of cattle. No trace, however, of either Boers or cattle was found there.

The columns comprising the drive southward were in constant communication with each other by signalling. Plumer's column was immediately on Kitchener's right, holding the line of the Oliphant's River, thus preventing the Boers, who were scattered in small groups in the bush veldt, from escaping in the direction of Pietersburg, whilst Park's column was operating on Kitchener's left, thus preventing the Boers breaking back towards Waterval and the Steenkampsberg mountains.

Gradually Kitchener's column moved southward, driving the Boers off the high ground and picking them up with their cattle and families in the low or bush veldt. To do this with greater effect the column was divided, one portion consisting of the battalion, one gun, the I.L.H. and Australians under Colonel Davies proceeding in a north-westerly direction to stop the Boers breaking back into the bush veldt in rear, whilst General Kitchener with the remainder of the column marched over the high ground overlooking the bush veldt, and on the direct road to the south. On the 22nd Davies' column reached Enkeldedoorn, whilst General Kitchener with the Rifle Brigade occupied Vaal Kop on the morning of the 23rd. On the first day out the mounted troops of Davies' force, scouring the bush in their advance, captured 23 prisoners, 8 wagons, 450 head of cattle, and 4000 sheep. They also brought in a number of families, some of whom had been hiding for months in kloofs and dongas in great fear of the Kaffirs. One woman with her children was seen weeping by the side of the track, and on being asked the reason, she implored that she also might be taken into the railway and not left behind. She was comforted by an assurance that the column would return and that she would be taken in.

Stores were now running short, and the biscuit and sugar rations were reduced to half.

In order to keep connection between the two portions of General Kitchener's column, two companies were left at Enkeldedoorn under the command of Captain Bartlett. These also formed a "stop" to prevent the Boers breaking back, and a post to which prisoners' families and cattle could be forwarded on their way to join the head-quarters at Paardeplaats, whither General Kitchener had gone from Vaal Kop.

The Regiment, with the Australian mounted troops, operating through dense bush proceeded in the direction of the Oliphant's River, capturing a considerable number of prisoners, cattle, wagons, and families, amongst the prisoners being Commandant Fourie.

Eight privates of the Regiment, who were escorting an ammunition cart, and who had lost their way, captured six Boers with all their cattle and brought them into camp.

When within twelve miles of the Oliphant's River, Davies, hearing that Commandant Schroeder with a small commando was directly between him and Plumer's column on the Oliphant's River, split his force into two. The infantry, comprising five companies of the Regiment, were sent back under Captain Jacson, with all the prisoners wagons and families to Enkeldedoorn, while Davies himself, with the Australians and one gun, started in pursuit of Schroeder. On nearing the Oliphant's River it was ascertained that Schroeder, with forty-one men and one Maxim gun and several wagons, had been forced by Davies' mounted troops across the river into the hands of Plumer, who had them in safe keeping.

Jacson's train of prisoners reached Enkeldedoorn on April 26th, and on the following day he received orders to proceed at once to Zuikerboschplaats and to take with him Bartlett's two companies from Enkeldedoorn. This place was reached at dusk, and shortly afterwards Davies brought up his Australians to the same camp, his column being then again united. The northern part of the bush veldt having been swept clear of Boers, Davies then moved due south and scoured the country round the Tafel Kop mountain, capturing a number of prisoners and wagons. Haartebeestfontein was reached late in the evening of the 28th, some of the companies of the Regiment having marched over hill and dale through thick scrub more than twenty miles. Four men had lost their way and were missing.

Orders were received on the following day from General Kitchener for Davies' force to rejoin head-quarters at Paardeplaats. An early start was made at 6 a.m. Lackau, 12½ miles, was reached at 11 a.m., and here the column halted and the cattle outspanned till 2.30 p.m. The heat in the bush veldt was excessive, and was very trying to the men and cattle. At 2.30 p.m. the march was again resumed, and after another ten miles Paardeplaats was reached at dusk.

It had been a hot and dusty march of 22½ miles, and the men and cattle were rather "done up." On arrival it was found that the General had moved on to Goedgedacht.

As soon as it was dark rockets were fired to try and direct the four missing men into camp, but without success.

On the following day the battalion with the Australians marched down the steep Zaaiplaats Pass to Buffelsvlei, bivouacking for the night on the banks of the Buffelsvlei River.

On arrival there it was again found that the General had moved on to Rooi Plaats, and that the 2nd Rifle Brigade had proceeded by the Tautesberg road with prisoners and families

A REGIMENT OF THE LINE

and cattle to Wonderfontein on the railway line.

May 1st found the force at Rooi Plaats, and here a halt was made on the 2nd. Two companies under Captain Bartlett were dispatched to Diepkloof and two companies under Captain Wren to Waterval in order to block the two roads to the north from the Botha's Berg, and to stop the Boers breaking back.

On May 3rd the Regiment with the Australian mounted infantry reached Waterval, and on the following day proceeded to Blinkwater. Two companies with two guns under Captain Ponsonby, R.A., were left behind to cover the retirement of some mounted infantry, with orders to rejoin in the evening.

General Blood, with the whole of his personal command, had left Blinkwater on the previous day for Middleburg, and on the 5th General Kitchener received orders to follow him. The column marched that day to Rooi Kop, twelve miles distant on the Middleburg road, and on the following day two companies Devon Regiment, two companies Rifle Brigade, five guns and one howitzer, with the sick, the whole under Captain Jacson, left for Bankfontein, where they were joined next morning by the remainder of General Kitchener's column.

At Bankfontein a telegram was received which announced that Major Davies had been promoted to the brevet rank of lieutenant-colonel, Major Curry granted a D.S.O., and Captain Jacson was to be promoted to the brevet rank of lieutenant-colonel on attaining the rank of major.

A halt was made at Bankfontein from the 8th till the 11th, when the force refitted, and on May the 12th the column marched to Rondebosch on the outskirts of Middleburg.

In the early part of May, 1901, a further drive on a large scale was organized by headquarters. This was intended to traverse the whole of the Eastern Transvaal south of the railway. The columns were to be extended from Middleburg through Carolina up to the Swazi border on the east, and then, with a circling movement based on Middleburg, gradually to sweep the country through Ermelo towards Bethel. Having rounded up all this country, the drive, extending from Bethel on the south to the Pretoria-Lorenzo railway on the north, was by a combined movement to the west-

A REGIMENT OF THE LINE 191

ward, to push all the Boers remaining in this part of the country with their cattle on to Johannesburg-Springs and the Pretoria-Standerton railway lines, which were guarded. The movement was under the direction of Sir Bindon Blood, and his forces consisted of eight columns.

The battalion found itself again under the command of General Walter Kitchener, forming part of his column, which was composed of the following troops :—

    1st Devonshire Regiment.
    2nd Rifle Brigade.
    6th West Australians (450 strong).
    2nd I.L.H. (800 strong).
    Four guns 53rd Field Battery R.A.
    One 5-inch gun.
    One naval 12-pounder.

Its position in the drive was on the left or outside edge of the circle of the operations.

The forces were put in motion on the 13th May, on which day Kitchener, advancing in the direction of the Swazi border, marched to Zaaiplaats ($12\frac{1}{2}$ miles), and thence without incident through Riet Kuil, reaching Schoonora on the 15th. In the neighbourhood of Schoonora Commandant Trichardt, with 170 of his followers, was surprised by the Australian mounted infantry, who killed one Boer and captured 300 head of cattle. A considerable number of Boers were reported to be in the neighbourhood.

The drifts over which the column had to pass after leaving Riet Kuil were bad, and only two companies reached Schoonora that night. The remainder of the battalion, which was rear-guard to the column, bivouacked with the baggage three miles out of camp near a branch of the Klein Oliphants River, and joined up with the column next morning. The following day Mooiplaats was reached, when a large number of cattle and some families were taken.

On May 16th the column moved to Grobellars Recht. Here the Boers were found in large numbers under Botha. The 5th and 6th West Australians whilst operating on the right flank of the column were ambushed, losing one officer and six men killed and thirteen wounded. The Boers were very truculent and gave considerable trouble, and the force was not in camp till dark. It was not, however, disturbed during the night.

The column left Grobellars Recht on the 16th with the 5th and 6th West Australians as rear-guard, supported by the Devonshire Regiment. The Boers followed up smartly for some hours, but there were no casualties, and camp was reached at Kromkrans at about 4 p.m. Smutsoog was reached the next day. On the march Pulteney's column, which was seen in the distance, mistaking Kitchener's column for a commando of Boers, shelled them with field guns. Their shooting was accurate, and it was not till General Kitchener threatened to send a 5-inch shell at them that they desisted. Fortunately no damage was done. From Smutsoog the column proceeded to Goedevervachting, a few Boers sniping the column on the march.

Much inconvenience was experienced from the cold, as it froze hard every night.

On the 20th the column marched to Florence, passing Bothwell and Lake Chrissie, and on the following day reached Veltevreden. Here the 2nd Rifle Brigade and the West

Australians left the column. On the march to Veltevreden a few Boers were seen, and there was some firing at the rear-guard.

On the following day a short march brought the force to Uitkyk, where a halt was made on the 23rd.

On the 24th the column on its march to Schapenberg captured 800 cattle and 4000 sheep, and five Boers surrendered.

A halt was made on the 25th and 26th at Schapenberg. Here 16,000 sheep, which were being driven along with the column, were slaughtered. These, daily increasing in number, hampered the movements of the rear-guard on the march to such an extent, that it was found impossible to drive them on to the railway; they were therefore slaughtered.

Lekkerloop was reached on the 27th, on which day the I.L.H. captured twenty-two prisoners. A halt was made at Lekkerloop from the 28th to 31st, during which time the I.L.H. under Colonel Mackenzie were busy capturing prisoners and clearing the country.

On June 1st the column marched to Bushman's Kop, proceeding on the following day to Vierwonden, crossing the Theespruit *en*

A REGIMENT OF THE LINE

route. The I.L.H. brought six prisoners into camp with them. The main column halted at Vierwonden from the 3rd till the 8th, whilst Captain Bartlett left for Hoilake on the 3rd in command of three companies as escort to a convoy, and on the 4th Captain Wren was ordered with one company and five guns to Bonnybraes. On the 9th the column marched to Bonnybraes, Colonel Mackenzie and the I.L.H. bringing in eighteen Boers and about 400 cattle and some families.

A halt was made at Bonnybraes on the 10th. The column was reunited on the 11th at Fernyhaugh, and on the 12th marched to Busby, the march being greatly delayed by a bad drift over the Umpolosi River. Ring Kink was reached on the 13th, and Woodstock on the 14th. Thirty Boer rifles were found on Woodstock Farm.

The column was then divided. Seven companies of the Regiment under Lieutenant-Colonel Davies, with the 2nd I.L.H. and the 5th and 6th West Australians, left Woodstock at 1 a.m., the remainder of the column proceeding, under General Kitchener's personal command, further south towards Bank Kop to round up some Boers reported in that neighbourhood.

Davies' mounted troops captured during the day fourteen Boers, some families, 100 cattle, 1000 sheep, and six wagons. This column marched twenty-two miles and camped for the night at Blaukrans, where Colonel Davies rested his men on the 16th.

Colbank was reached on the 17th, when all mounted troops left to join Kitchener's column at Bank Kop.

The following day the Regiment marched to Kranspan and joined up with General Kitchener. The column captured that day several families and twenty-two Boers. On the 19th the whole column marched in the direction of Ermelo, and camped for the night on a hill overlooking the town. Camp was reached at nightfall after a very long, dusty, and tiring march, the rear-guard getting in after dark.

On the 20th the force marched through Ermelo to Driehook. A number of Boers followed up the rear-guard, and there was a good deal of firing, but no casualties. The march was resumed on the following day and

Kranspoort was reached. On the 22nd the column marched to Witbank, the rear-guard being engaged almost the whole march. A halt was made at Witbank. The West Australians were here again ambushed, losing two men killed, one officer and two men wounded, and five taken prisoners.

Three hundred Boers were reported on the left flank at nightfall, and preparations were made to receive a night attack, which, however, did not come off. On the following day a dense fog delayed the march till 9 a.m., and it was not till late that Vaal Bank was reached. The rear-guard, consisting of the Devon Regiment and the 6th West Australians, was engaged the whole day with the Boers, who followed the column right up to the new camp. That night the whole Regiment was on outpost duty.

The rear-guard was engaged heavily the following day during the march to Bankpan.

Campbell's and Babington's columns were on the immediate right. The Devons halted for the day at Bankpan, when the 5th and 6th West Australians left to join Campbell's column at Middlekraal, the 18th Hussars exchanging over to Kitchener's column.

A night march was made on the 26th for the purpose of surrounding a farm some eight miles distant. This was accomplished by midnight. No Boers were taken. The column halted till daylight, when the march was again resumed, and Erstegeluk reached in the afternoon. A number of Boers were surprised in the neighbouring farms by the mounted troops; and shortly after camp was formed, a body of Boers attempted to drive in the outposts and to attack the camp, but without success.

The following day Bethel was reached, and camp was formed close to Colonel Babington's column. The 18th Hussars, reconnoitring to the south-east of Bethel, were surprised by a large party of Boers. Lieutenant Green, Devonshire Regiment, who was in charge of the Colt gun attached to the 18th Hussars and which was manned by men of the Devonshire Regiment, behaved very gallantly in bringing his gun at once into action and engaging the Boers within a range of 500 yards, thus covering the cavalry and giving them time to rally.

A REGIMENT OF THE LINE

On June 29th the march was resumed, and the column reached Schurvekop, the rearguard receiving a good deal of attention from the Boers. Camp was formed at Middlekraal on the following day. Here Campbell's column was again met with.

Middlekraal was left on July 1st, and the column marched in the direction of Springs. A number of Boers were in the vicinity of the first camp, Witbank, and the camp was sniped during the night. The following day the column marched to Bakenlaagte, the scene of the disaster to Benson's column, the rearguard being followed up by a few Boers.

After a short march the following day Grootpan was reached, and at 8 p.m. three companies of the Regiment under Captain Bartlett, and the 5th and 6th West Australians, made a night march to the south, capturing a picquet of six Boers early next morning. The column, after a twelve-miles' march, reached Sondagskraal on the 4th at 1 p.m. On arrival there news was received that a Boer convoy, accompanied by Louis Botha, was in the neighbourhood of Trichardtsfontein, about fifteen miles from Sondagskraal.

General Kitchener determined to intercept this convoy, and for this reason the following force under his personal command, viz. two squadrons 19th Hussars, 5th and 6th West Australians, and four companies of the Devonshire Regiment under Captain Jacson, set out the same evening. The mounted troops of Colville's column co-operated. Trichardtsfontein was reached an hour before dawn, when the place was found deserted. A halt was made there for the day, when Colville's column left.

At nightfall several Boers were seen on the hills in the vicinity, and there was every reason to suppose that a night attack was contemplated by them. Preparations were made accordingly, but the night was passed quietly.

At dawn the return march was commenced. The Boers attacked the rear-guard before it left camp and before it was formed up, and engaged it the whole way back to Sondagskraal, until finally they came under fire of the 5-inch gun in position in that camp.

During the preceding thirty-one hours the four companies of the Regiment had marched forty-two miles.

DAWN—AFTER A NIGHT MARCH, TRICHARDTSFONTEIN

A REGIMENT OF THE LINE

Whilst this enterprise was being undertaken the remainder of the battalion, with the transport of the column, had remained at Sondagskraal under Colonel Davies.

On the 7th the force marched to Goedehoop, and proceeding without incident on the 8th to Brakfontein, on the 9th to Strypan, reached Springs on the 10th. The last two marches were long and tiring, and what little strength was left in the oxen was exhausted. The men likewise required a rest and a refit after their long trek from Lydenburg, which had extended through Secoconi's country in the Northern Transvaal, down south to Middleburg, thence east to the Swazi border and over the Eastern Transvaal, reaching as far south as Bethel, to Springs, near Johannesburg. Eighty per cent of the men had on arrival at Springs neither shirts nor socks, and the bitter cold of the high veldt pierced keenly through the thin Indian khaki drill. The column required generally doing up before again "taking the floor." It was expected by all that the infantry at least would be relieved by a fresh battalion.

But it was not to be, for General Walter

Kitchener insisted on the Devons accompanying him, and his column set out again from Springs on the 14th on a trek to the north, and without much fighting or incident reached Middleburg on July 22nd. The country through which the column passed was cleared of everything living, including Kaffirs.

Three days' halt was allowed the column at Middleburg, and on the 25th a start was again made for the north. It was now composed as under :—

Four guns 81st Field Battery R.A., under Major Simpson.
One pompom.
19th Hussars.
5th and 6th West Australians.
Half company Scottish Horse.
Half company Mounted Infantry.
Seven companies Devonshire Regiment.

Two companies under Captain Bartlett had left on the 24th July to garrison Elands River station, on the Pretoria-Lorenzo railway.

The seven companies with General Kitchener marched out 723 strong.

Two other columns were operating with

A REGIMENT OF THE LINE 203

General Kitchener, one under Colonel Park and the other under Colonel Campbell. The whole were under the supreme command of General Walter Kitchener.

On the first day out the 19th Hussars captured a pompom and about sixty prisoners of Ben Viljoen's and Muller's commandos after a very gallant little action in which five men of the 19th Hussars especially distinguished themselves. A great number of cattle and many wagons were also taken, and the Boers lost about twelve killed and twenty wounded.

General Walter Kitchener's column encamped at Rooi Kraal for a few days before moving to a camp at Diep Kloof, from which place convoys were sent to the railway for stores for the three columns.

The first of these convoys under Lieutenant-Colonel Jacson left on August 1st, marched to Middleburg, by Blinkwater and Elandslaagte, and reached Middleburg in three days; halted one day there to load up, and returned via Elandslaagte and Noitgedacht to Diepkloof in three more days, receiving on their return the congratulations of General Kitchener on their performance.

On the 10th another convoy, again under Lieutenant-Colonel Jacson, with an escort composed of men of the Devons and Leicesters and some Scottish mounted infantry and two field guns, started for Wonderfontein.

This convoy consisted of all the wagons of the columns of Colonels Park and Campbell and General Kitchener, which had to be filled up at the railway line and brought back.

Waterval was reached on the 10th, Rhenoster Hoek on the 11th, Sterkloop on the 12th, Uitflucht on the 13th, and Wonderfontein on the 14th. Slight opposition was met with, and three Boers were captured with wagons containing a quantity of grain.

The convoy having halted and loaded up on the 15th, started on its return journey on the 16th.

The journey to Wonderfontein had been up the Steelpoort valley, and the road had been found difficult. It was very much intersected with water-courses running off the high veldt, and these necessitated frequent halts to allow of the passage of the wagons in single file, and the reclosing up of the convoy after crossing.

A different road over the high veldt, thus avoiding the water-courses, was chosen for the return journey, and it was perhaps fortunate that this new road was selected, as it was reported afterwards that Ben Viljoen had taken up a position at the time in the Steelpoort valley to intercept the return column.

On the 16th the convoy marched to Panplaats; on the 17th to Roedekop (where some of Viljoen's men were met with and some more of his grain carts captured), Blinkwater on the 18th, and Diepkloof on the 19th.

After a few days' scouring of the country round Diepkloof and the valley towards the Oliphants River, the three columns concentrated at Blinkwater. Here an entrenched camp was formed under the command of Lieutenant-Colonel Jacson, consisting of the baggage of the three columns, the hospitals, and most of the field guns, with a garrison included amongst which were four companies of the Regiment.

Park's and Campbell's columns marched east into the hills in the Ohrigstadt direction, Park penetrating almost as far as Pilgrim's Rest, while General Kitchener's column moved south towards Middleburg. On September 3rd the force was broken up, Colonel Park's column being left in the neighbourhood of Blinkwater, whilst General Kitchener's column marched towards the railway at Wonderfontein, which was reached on September 5th.

On arrival at Wonderfontein it was found that trekking was for the time being, finished. Orders were received for the Regiment to entrain for Machadodorp for the purpose of garrisoning the railway blockhouses.

The General's farewell order to the Regiment on its leaving the column with which it had been so long associated was as follows :—

"COLUMN ORDER BY MAJOR-GENERAL F. W. KITCHENER

"*Wonderfontein, September 5th,* 1901.

"It has been the privilege of the Major-General to include the 1st Devon Regiment in his command since the relief of Ladysmith, and it is with great regret that he has now to part with the last fighting unit of the 7th Brigade. The reputation earned by the Regiment at Elandslaagte and Ladysmith is a matter of history. Since that time this excellent corps has fought and marched in summer rain and winter frost during many long months, through the length and breadth of the Eastern Transvaal.

"The face of the country will remain for many years scarred with the trenches they have dug and the works they have made. They have proved on all occasions what a sound regimental system worked by thoroughly sound officers, N.C.O.s, and men can do.

"The Major-General and all in number one column wish the Devons good luck and a pleasant time in the near future."

On September 6th the Regiment entrained. The General and his staff and the whole column turned out to give the Regiment a hearty farewell. Machadodorp was reached at about 2 p.m., and all the posts round the town were taken over from the Royal Irish Fusiliers. The railway blockhouses in the neighbourhood of Machadodorp were also taken over. Colonel Davies was appointed commandant of the station, and Captain Ravenshaw station staff officer.

During September and October six companies were located on the Lydenburg road as far as Witklip, holding the following posts:— Helvetia, Schwartzkop, Schoeman's Kloof, Badfontein, and Witklip. Two companies remained at Machadodorp with the battalion head-quarters.

In October, one company under Captain Holland and Lieutenant Willis, whilst acting as escort to a party erecting blockhouses in the Badfontein valley, was attacked by Ben Viljoen and about three hundred Boers. The Boers galloped down from the hills on to the extended company. The men behaved with great gallantry, and finally, after a sharp and mixed-up fight, drove off the Boers. One man of the company fell into their hands and was stripped and left. Lieutenant Willis, for gallantry on this occasion, was rewarded with the D.S.O., and Lance-Corporal Cummings was promoted corporal by the Commander-in-Chief for gallantry in the field.

During the first week of November, orders were received for the 1st Battalion to proceed to Standerton *en route* to India. The 2nd Battalion had been quartered there for a con-

DEVONS EN ROUTE TO DURBAN

A REGIMENT OF THE LINE

siderable time, and a transfer of men was effected from one battalion to the other. The two battalions spent Christmas together.

On January 1st (1902) the 1st Battalion entrained at daylight for Durban.

The battalion met with a great reception at Maritzburg, where a halt was made for nine hours. Here each man was presented by the ladies of that place with a pipe, half a pound of tobacco, and a pockethandkerchief.

The battalion sailed from South Africa for India, with the following officers and 922 rank and file :—

Bt. Lieutenant-Colonel T. A. H. Davies, D.S.O.
Bt. Lieutenant-Colonel M. G. Jacson.
Captain E. C. Wren.
    ,,   T. C. B. Holland.
    ,,   G. H. I. Graham.
Lieutenant T. B. Harries.
    ,,   G. I. Watts.
    ,,   D. H. Blunt.
    ,,   H. R. Gunning.
    ,,   S. T. Hailey.
    ,,   H. W. F. Twiss.

Lieutenant E. S. C. Willis.
„ W. E. Scafe.
„ G. F. A. Kane.
2nd Lieutenant C. Edward-Collins.
„ „ M. D. Young.
„ „ C. W. Hext.
„ „ A. M. Mills.
„ „ R. C. Wrey.

Brevet-Major and Adjutant H. S. L. Ravenshaw.

Of the above, it may be noted that the following left India with the battalion in 1899 :—

Bt. Lieut.-Colonel M. G. Jacson.

Captain E. C. Wren.
„ G. H. I. Graham.

Lieutenant T. B. Harries.
„ G. I. Watts.
„ D. H. Blunt.
„ H. R. Gunning.
„ S. T. Hayley.
„ H. W. F. Twiss.

Bt.-Major and Adjutant H. S. L. Ravenshaw.

A REGIMENT OF THE LINE

The following officers of the battalion remained behind in South Africa :—

Colonel C. W. Park, A.D.C., commanding a column.

Captain and Bt.-Major E. M. Morris, South African Constabulary.

Captain Bartlett, D.A.A.G. for Intelligence.
„ Vyvyan, Provost Marshal, Barberton.
„ Travers, South African Constabulary.

Lieutenant-General Lyttleton met the battalion at Howick on its way to Durban, and wished them "farewell."

The following telegram was received at Durban from Lord Kitchener, commanding the forces in South Africa :—

"To O. C. 1st Devon Regiment,
　　　　　　　　　Durban.
"From Lord Kitchener,
　　　　　　　　　Johannesburg.

" Please express to officers and men of the Regiment under your command my high appreciation of their services in South Africa during the war, which has already enhanced the great reputation of the Regiment. In bidding you good-bye, I associate myself with all your comrades remaining in the country in hearty wishes for your future good luck."

It should be added to the records of the battalion, which throughout two years and three months had fought and marched incessantly in South Africa, that it had never once experienced the slightest trace of an " unfortunate incident," and had during that time lost only three prisoners of war, two of whom lost their way in the dark at Geluk and marched into enemy's lines, the third having been taken during the company fight in the Badfontein valley against 300 of Ben Viljoen's men. The miles traversed by the battalion in the long continuous treks during the war are summarized as under. The miles are measured off the map simply from place to place and from camp to camp, and they do not include the distances marched in fighting, flanking, or other movements, or in convoy work and expeditions in the Lydenburg district, which, if included, would probably double the distance marched.

A REGIMENT OF THE LINE

Trek under Sir Redvers Buller.

August 7th till October 2nd, 1900.

Zandspruit to Lydenburg, 271 miles in 54 days, including all halts.

Trek under General Walter Kitchener.

April 13th till September 2nd, 1901.

Lydenburg, Secoconi's country, Middleburg, Swazi Border, Bethel, Springs, Middleburg, Bothas Berg, and country north of the railway line. 1006 miles in 141 days, including all halts.

On the evening of January 1st the Regiment embarked on the s.s. *Armenian*, and was followed by the 2nd battalion Gordon Highlanders, who embarked on January 2nd.

On January 3rd the ship conveying the two regiments sailed for Bombay, which port was reached on January 18th.

Lord Northcote, the Governor of Bombay, received the two regiments on disembarkation and addressed them, congratulating them on their good work in South Africa.

The Devons entrained the same evening for Shahjehanpur in the United Provinces.

THE RECORD OF

The honours gained by the officers and men of the battalion were as follows :—

1. Colonel Yule to be C.B.
2. Lieutenant-Colonel Park to be Brevet-Colonel and Aide-de-Camp to the King.
3. Major Davies, D.S.O., to be Brevet Lieutenant-Colonel.
4. Major Curry granted D.S.O.
5. Captain Jacson to be Brevet Lieutenant-Colonel on promotion to the rank of Major.
6. Captain Norton Goodwyn, D.S.O., to be Brevet Lieutenant-Colonel on promotion to the rank of Major.
7. Captain Travers granted D.S.O.
8. Captain and Adjutant Ravenshaw to be Brevet-Major.
9. Captain Masterson to be Brevet-Major and awarded the Victoria Cross.
10. Captain E. M. Morris to be Brevet-Major.
11. Lieutenant Emerson granted D.S.O.
12.   „   Willis granted D.S.O.

A REGIMENT OF THE LINE

Attached Officers.

13. Lieutenant Tringham, the Queen's, granted D.S.O.
14. Lieutenant Cowie, Dorset Regiment, granted D.S.O.

The following officers of the 1st Battalion were mentioned in dispatches :—

Colonel Yule—once.

Brevet-Colonel Park, A.D.C.—twice.

Brevet Lieutenant-Colonel Davies, D.S.O.—twice.

Brevet Lieutenant-Colonel Jacson—twice.

,, ,, Goodwyn—twice.

Major Curry, D.S.O.—twice.

Brevet-Major Ravenshaw—four times.

,, Masterson, V.C.—twice.

Captain W. B. Lafone—twice.

,, Bartlett—once.
,, Travers, D.S.O.—once.
,, Wren—once.
,, Smyth-Osbourne—twice.
,, Luxmore—once.

Lieutenant Field—twice.

,, Emerson, D.S.O.—three times.

Lieutenant Willis, D.S.O.—once.
    ,,   Tringham, D.S.O. (attached)—once
    ,,   Cowie, D.S.O. (attached)—twice.
    ,,   Twiss—once.
    ,,   Harris—once.
    ,,   Green—once.
    ,,   Watts—once.
    ,,   Gardiner—once.

Non-commissioned Officers and Men.

The following were granted Distinguished Conduct Medals :—

Colour-Sergeant Payne.
        ,,   Horswell.
        ,,   Palmer.
        ,,   Burnell.
        ,,   Webb.
        ,,   Aplin.
Sergeant Pitt.
    ,,   Downing.
    ,,   Hudson.
    ,,   Williams.
Lance-Sergeant Poulter.
        ,,   Young.
        ,,   Rowe.

A REGIMENT OF THE LINE

Corporal Hansford.
Private Boulton.
„ Davies.

The following non-commissioned officers and men were mentioned in dispatches:—

Colour-Sergeant Palmer—four times.
„ Payne—twice.
„ Horswell—once.
„ Burnell—once.
„ Webb—once.
„ Burchell—once.

Sergeant Hudson—once.
„ Downing—once.
„ Young—twice.
„ Poulter—once.
„ Curtis—once.

Lance-Sergeant Rowe—twice.

Corporal Hayes—once (promoted sergeant).

Lance-Corporal Cummings—once (promoted corporal).

Private Brimicombe—twice.
„ Norman—three times.
„ Cox—twice.
„ Smith—once.

Private Youlden—once.
„ Clay—once.
„ Edwards—once.
„ Hayman—once.
„ Davies—once.
„ Hansford—twice.
„ Boulton—once.

The following is a list of the killed and wounded and of those who died of disease during the campaign :—

Officers: Killed.

Captain W. B. Lafone.
Lieutenant Field.
„ Dalzel.
„ Price-Dent.
2nd Lieutenant Cumin.
„ Carey.
Lieutenant Walker, Somerset Light Infantry (attached).

Wounded.

Captain Lafone—twice.
„ Masterson.
„ Luxmore.
2nd Lieutenant Twiss.

MONUMENT ERECTED IN LADYSMITH CEMETERY

A REGIMENT OF THE LINE

2nd Lieutenant Scafe.
  „   Kane.
Lieutenant Caffin (attached).
  „   Tringham (attached).
  „   Byrne (attached).
2nd Lieutenant Gunning.
  „   Hayley.
  „   Green.

N.C.O.'s and Men.
Killed and died of wounds and diseases.

Private Taylor, died of disease Ladysmith.
  „   Forman, killed Ladysmith.
  „   Salter   „   „
  „   Nolloth, died of disease Ladysmith.
  „   Richards „   „   „
  „   Edwards   „   „   „
  „   Paddon   „   „   Transvaal.
  „   Hayward   „   „   „
  „   Morgan, died of wounds „
  „   Manley, died of disease „
  „   Goff, killed Transvaal.
  „   Brockett, killed Ladysmith.
  „   Cook, died of disease Ladysmith.
  „   Banfield, died of wounds Ladysmith.
  „   Sullivan, died of disease „

Private Woolacott, died of disease Transvaal.
" Penfold " " "
" Silvester " " Ladysmith.
" Marsh " " "
" Nunn " " "

Lance-Corporal Leonard, died of disease Ladysmith.

Private Evans, died of disease Ladysmith.
" Parrott, killed Transvaal.
" Arthur, died of disease Transvaal.
" Luck " " "
" Mathews " " "
" Clements " " Ladysmith.
" Seager, died of wounds "
" Connabeer, died of disease "
" Swannell " " "

Lance-Corporal Spear, died of disease.

Private Litton, killed Ladysmith.
" Vinnicombe, died of disease.
" Down " "
" Rowland " "

Lance-Corporal Pratt, killed Ladysmith.

Private Bibb, killed Ladysmith.
" Harvey " "
" Woods, died of wounds received Ladysmith.

A REGIMENT OF THE LINE

Private Hornsby, died of wounds received Ladysmith.

Private Milton, died of disease Ladysmith.
- ,, Firminger ,, ,, ,,
- ,, Vicary ,, ,, ,,
- ,, Newbury ,, ,, ,,
- ,, Lane ,, ,, ,,
- ,, Sheridan ,, ,, ,,
- ,, Horswell ,, ,, ,,

Lance-Corporal Vern, killed Ladysmith.

Private Bamsey, killed Ladysmith.
- ,, Fair ,, ,,
- ,, Roper ,, ,,
- ,, Davidson ,, ,,
- ,, Curtis ,, ,,
- ,, Marden ,, ,,
- ,, Brown ,, ,,
- ,, Newcombe ,, ,,

Lance-Corporal Pigeon, died of wounds received Ladysmith.

Private Bevan, died of wounds received Ladysmith.

Private Page, died of wounds received Ladysmith.

Private Vern, died of disease.

Private Rosser died of disease.
   ,, Clotworthy ,, ,,
   ,, Turner ,, ,,
   ,, Ponting ,, ,,
   ,, Rawbone ,, ,,
   ,, Jeffries, died of wounds.
   ,, Young, died of disease.
   ,, Davidson ,, ,,
   ,, Cunningham ,, ,,
Lance-Corporal Murfin, died of disease.
Private Livermore ,, ,,
Corporal Wright ,, ,,
Private Humphrey, killed.
   ,, Bowles, died of disease.
   ,, Watts ,, ,,
   ,, Meade ,, ,,
   ,, Phillips ,, ,,
   ,, Kingham ,, ,,
   ,, Winsor, killed Reitfontein.
   ,, Mayne, died of disease.
   ,, Tayler ,, ,,
   ,, Pike ,, ,,
   ,, Trenchard ,, ,,
   ,, Salter, killed Geluk.
   ,, Cole ,, ,,
   ,, Mcgrath ,, ,,

A REGIMENT OF THE LINE

Private Smith, killed Geluk.
    ,,   Lashbrook, died of wounds.
    ,,   Rowe, died of disease.
    ,,   Holmes ,,   ,,
    ,,   Conian ,,   ,,

N.C.O.'s and Men Wounded.

Private Bidwell.	Private Lock.
,, Turner.	,, Hutchings.
,, Pirouet.	,, Bevan.
,, Spiller.	,, Orchard.
,, Laycock.	,, Spreadbury.
,, Wright.	,, Barnett.
Col.-Sergeant Webb.	,, Cox.
Corporal Shapland.	,, Hay.
,, Bradford.	,, Page.
Lance-Corporal Millward.	,, King.
	,, Saunders.
Lance-Corporal Bennet.	,, Wheaton.
	,, Stapley.
Lance-Corporal Whitman.	,, Brazil.
	,, West.
Private Cox.	,, Onyett.
,, Norman.	,, Winson.
,, Palmer.	,, Dudley.
,, Webber.	,, Lott.
,, Lemon.	,, Hornsby.

Private Fordham.
„ Turner.
„ Varndell.
„ Mower.
„ Taylor.
Colour-Sergeant Burchell.
Sergeant Williams.
„ Hawkins.
Corporal Lovell.
„ Saunders.
Private Lupton.
„ Harford.
„ Parrott.
„ Mahoney.
„ Allen.
„ Curtiss.
„ O'Brien.
„ Brown.
„ Gray.
„ Anstey.
„ Lucas.
Sergeant Leach.
Private Capp.
„ Gander.

Private Gregory.
„ Reynolds.
„ Devitte.
„ Osmonde.
„ Burge.
„ Newton.
„ Reed.
Lance-Corporal Bromford—twice.
Private Rowe.
„ Sussex.
„ Ward.
„ Smith.
„ Easton.
„ Legatt.
Col.-Sergeant Palmer.
Private Bray.
Lance-Corporal Spear.
Private Kean.
„ Welch.
„ Peckham.
Lance-Corpl. Quick.
Private Burns.
„ Simmons.
„ Palmer.

Total number of killed and wounded and died of disease :—

A REGIMENT OF THE LINE

	Killed and died of disease.	Wounded.
Officers	7	12
N.C.O.'s and men	91	85
Total casualties		195

A large memorial is erected to the memory of those who fell on January 6th at Wagon Hill, Ladysmith, on the spot where the charge took place. It bears the following inscription:

To the glory of God,
and in memory of
the following Officers, Non-Commissioned Officers,
and Men of the
1st Battalion Devonshire Regiment,
who fell in the gallant and
successful charge made across this
place by three companies during the
fight on 6th January, 1900.
Siege of Ladysmith.

Captain W. B. Lafone.
Lieutenant H. N. Field.
Lance-Corpl. J. Pigeon.
,, ,, W. D. Pratt.
,, ,, A. Vern.
Private T. Bamsey.
,, A. Bevan.
,, J. Bibb.
,, W. Brown.
,, A. Curtis.
,, W. Davidson.

Private W. Fair.
,, W. Harvey.
,, E. Hornsby.
,, T. Litton.
,, H. Marden.
,, W. Newcombe.
,, F. W. J. Page.
,, G. Roper.
,, J. Seager.
,, W. Woods.

Lieutenant E. E. M. Walker, Somerset Light Infantry
(attached).
"Semper Fidelis."

A marble monument is erected in Ladysmith cemetery to those who were killed or died of disease during the siege of Ladysmith, and their names are recorded on it. A small iron cross was also placed at the head of the grave of every man of the Regiment who was killed or who died of disease during the war.

These memorials were erected by the officers, non-commissioned officers, and men of the 1st Battalion Devonshire Regiment, to the memory of their gallant comrades.

www.ingramcontent.com/pod-product-compliance
Lightning Source LLC
Chambersburg PA
CBHW052047220426
43663CB00012B/2470